James Forman and SNCC

Lucent Library of Black History

Michael V. Uschan

LUCENT BOOKS

A part of Gale, Cengage Learning

GALE
CENGAGE Learning

Detroit • New York • San Francisco • New Haven, Conn • Waterville, Maine • London

LIBRARY OF CONGRESS CATALOGING-IN-PUBLICATION DATA

Uschan, Michael V., 1948-
 James Forman and SNCC / by Michael V. Uschan.
   p. cm. -- (Lucent library of Black history)
 Includes bibliographical references and index.
 ISBN 978-1-4205-0920-5 (hardcover)
1. Forman, James, 1928-2005--Juvenile literature. 2. Student Nonviolent Coordinating Committee (U.S.)--Juvenile literature. 3. Civil rights workers--United States--Biography--Juvenile literature. 4. African American civil rights workers--Biography--Juvenile literature. 5. African Americans--Civil rights--History--20th century--Juvenile literature. 6. Civil rights movements--United States--History--20th century--Juvenile literature. I. Title.
 E185.97.F715U63 2013
 323.092--dc23
 [B]
                                                        2012050154

Lucent Books
27500 Drake Rd.
Farmington Hills, MI 48331

ISBN-13: 978-1-4205-0920-5
ISBN-10: 1-4205-0920-9

Contents

Foreword

It has been more than 500 years since Africans were first brought to the New World in shackles, and over 140 years since slavery was formally abolished in the United States. Over 50 years have passed since the fallacy of "separate but equal" was obliterated in the American courts, and some 40 years since the watershed Civil Rights Act of 1964 guaranteed the rights and liberties of all Americans, especially those of color. Over time, these changes have become celebrated landmarks in American history. In the twenty-first century, African American men and women are politicians, judges, diplomats, professors, deans, doctors, artists, athletes, business owners, and home owners. For many, the scars of the past have melted away in the opportunities that have been found in contemporary society. Observers such as Peter N. Kirsanow, who sits on the U.S. Commission of Civil Rights, point to these accomplishments and conclude, "The growing black middle class may be viewed as proof that most of the civil rights battles have been won."

In spite of these legal victories, however, prejudice and inequality have persisted in American society. In 2003, African Americans comprised just 12 percent of the nation's population, yet accounted for 44 percent of its prison inmates and 24 percent of its poor. Racially motivated hate crimes continue to appear on the pages of major newspapers in many American cities. Furthermore, many African Americans still experience either overt or muted racism in their daily lives. A 1996 study undertaken by Professor Nancy Krieger of the Harvard School of Public Health, for example, found that 80 percent of the African American participants reported having experienced racial discrimination in one or more settings, including at work or school, applying for housing and medical care, from the police or in the courts, and on the street or in a public setting.

It is for these reasons that many believe the struggle for racial equality and justice is far from over. These episodes of discrimination threaten to shatter the illusion that America has completely overcome its racist past, causing many black Americans to become increasingly frustrated and confused. Scholar and writer Ellis Cose has described this splintered state in the following way: "I have done everything I was supposed to do. I have stayed out of trouble with the law, gone to the right schools, and worked myself nearly to death. What more do they want? Why in God's name won't they accept me as a full human being?" For Cose and others, the struggle for equality and justice has yet to be fully achieved.

In many subtle yet important ways the traumatic experiences of slavery and segregation continue to inform the way race is discussed and experienced in the twenty-first century. Indeed, it is possible that America will always grapple with the fallout from its distressing past. Ulric Haynes, dean of the Hofstra University School of Business, has said, "Perhaps race will always matter, given the historical circumstances under which we came to this country." But studying this past and understanding how it contributes to present-day dialogues about race and history in America is a critical component of contemporary education. To this end, the Lucent Library of Black History offers a thorough look at the experiences that have shaped the black community and the American people as a whole. Annotated bibliographies provide readers with ideas for further research, while fully documented primary and secondary source quotations enhance the text. Each book in the series explores a different episode of black history; together they provide students with a wealth of information as well as launching points for further study and discussion.

Introduction

SNCC's Organizer

The Student Nonviolent Coordinating Committee (SNCC) operated for less than a decade. But during its brief yet historic existence during the 1960s, it was perhaps the most effective organization ever created to help African Americans secure the civil rights that institutionalized southern racism and white supremacy had long denied them. SNCC—both its allies and enemies alike referred to it verbally as SNICK—grew out of a wave of protests that began on February 1, 1960, when four black college students sat down at a lunch counter in Greensboro, North Carolina, that was reserved for whites. When a waitress refused to serve them, they sat quietly until the restaurant closed. They then returned the next day to continue their peaceful protest against Jim Crow, the racist system of segregation that denied them service.

Jim Crow, a systematic practice of discriminating against and segregating African Americans, had denied southern blacks many of their civil rights for nearly a century. Jim Crow laws in most southern states barred blacks from using restaurants, hotels, and other public businesses. After the Greensboro lunch counter sit-in in early 1960, the nonviolent sit-in tactic aimed at dismantling Jim Crow spread quickly to other southern cities even though hundreds of black and white protesters were arrested and beaten by racist police and civilians who feared African Americans might finally succeed in ending such blatant discrimination.

SNCC itself was born in April 1960, when more than two hundred college students involved in sit-ins, or interested in them, gathered at Shaw University in Raleigh, North Carolina. The students met so they could band together to coordinate their protests and make them more effective. They also wanted to consider other ways to fight for black rights. That Easter-weekend gathering attracted black and white students from northern schools as well as schools in the South. They decided to create SNCC, a group that vowed to use nonviolent measures to help southern blacks gain basic rights such as voting and to end the system of legalized racial segregation that had treated blacks as second-class citizens for nearly a century.

Howard Zinn, a history professor at Spelman College in Atlanta (the first institution of higher education for black women) and a SNCC adviser, documented the group's early history in his 1964 book *SNCC: The New Abolitionists*. Zinn, who was white, wrote that SNCC was unique in history because young people led it:

> For the first time in our history a major social movement, shaking the nation to its bones, is being led by youngsters. [These] young rebels call themselves the Student Nonviolent Coordinating Committee, but they are more a movement than an organization, for no bureaucratized structure can contain their spirit, no printed program capture the fierce and elusive quality of their thinking. And while they have no famous leaders, very little money, no inner access to the seats of national authority, they are clearly the front line of the Negro assault on [racism against blacks].[1]

In the past, older African Americans who were ministers, lawyers, and doctors had led the fight for civil rights. But college students, most of them still teenagers, were the heart and soul of SNCC, and its members included even younger students still in high school. In June 1960 Louis E. Lomax, the first African American television journalist, wrote that those young people had rejected the less militant tactics of their elders because they were tired of waiting for their rights. Lomax claimed that in just a few months of actively protesting against racism they had reenergized the fight for black rights that had been going on for several centuries and "completely reversed the power flow within the Negro community."[2]

Despite the dedication, tactical strategy, and bravery these young people had shown in challenging segregation, they needed guidance in organizing their ongoing war against racism. It was in that role that James Forman became perhaps the most important leader SNCC had ever had.

The Organizer

Forman was SNCC's executive secretary from 1961 to 1966, the period in which it experienced its greatest success in helping blacks achieve legal equality with whites. At the age of thirty-three when he joined SNCC, Forman was more than a decade older than most of the staff members and volunteers whose activities he would guide. In his history of SNCC, Clayborne Carson claimed that Forman "provided [the] administrative skill and political sophistication the young people needed to operate."[3]

One of Forman's tasks was to hire workers. SNCC had only sixteen staff members when Forman joined it in 1961, but by 1964 he had overseen the group's growth to more than 150 full-time workers. One of the first people Forman persuaded to work for SNCC was Julian Bond, a twenty-one-year-old student at Morehouse, a black college in Atlanta. As SNCC's communications director, Bond worked closely with Forman from 1961 through 1966. When Forman died on January 10, 2005, Bond praised him for how well he had managed SNCC operations and organized the group's activities: "He was indefatigable. It was said that on his deathbed, Frederick Douglass's last words were 'Organize! Organize!' That's what Forman did every day of his life."[4] A former slave, Douglass was one of the nineteenth century's most respected leaders in the fight for black rights.

Forman performed a wide variety of tasks to support SNCC's work. He organized protests, marches, and voter registration drives, tasks that were difficult and dangerous because of white violence directed against civil rights workers. He hired scores of field secretaries, the name for workers who led SNCC activities in various southern communities, found places for them to live, usually with local black families, and kept in contact with them to monitor their progress. Forman also raised money for SNCC, including cash to bail people out of jail when they were arrested,

James Forman was the executive secretary of the Student Nonviolent Coordinating Committee (SNCC) from 1961 to 1966, the period in which it saw its greatest success in helping blacks achieve legal equality with whites.

and was a liaison with federal government officials who sometimes helped in the fight for black rights.

Although Forman worked out of SNCC's national headquarters in Atlanta, he traveled extensively and participated in many historical events in the fight for civil rights, including the 1963 March on Washington and the protests in Selma, Alabama, in 1965 that led to new protections for blacks' voting rights. As a result of his work in the field, Forman was arrested, jailed, and beaten by racist police and white civilians who opposed black rights.

A Quiet Leader

Forman was a low-key leader despite the power he wielded as SNCC's executive secretary. In a story in the *New York Amsterdam News* on Forman's death in 2005, former SNCC worker George E. Curry noted that "Forman was more comfortable serving in the background of an organization brimming with youthful talent."[5] Many of the young people Forman directed became famous, including Bond, future Georgia congressman John Lewis, and Stokely Carmichael, who later changed his name to Kwame Ture. But they all owed part of their celebrity to Forman, whose steady guidance behind the scenes helped turn them into icons of the 1960s fight for civil rights.

Chapter One

James Forman

Although James Forman was born in Chicago on October 4, 1928, he lived in Marshall County, Mississippi, with his maternal grandmother for the first six years of his life. It was as a youngster in the South that Forman first encountered the cruel reality of racism. He once walked into a drugstore in Memphis, Tennessee, sat down at a marble-topped counter, and asked for a glass of soda. The man who served him told the young boy he could have soda in a can, not a glass, and that he could not sit at the counter to drink because he was black. The man also called him a degrading racial epithet. It was the first time the boy had heard the term, and this treatment made James cry. Another time, when James forgot to say "Yes, ma'am" to a clerk in a store, several white men told his uncle they would hurt the boy if he was not more respectful to whites in the future. The threats scared James, but when he got home his grandmother calmed him down by saying she would protect him.

Forman once explained simply that "those kinds of things are things I grew up with."[6] Such brushes with racism frightened Forman as a child, but they fueled his determination as an adult to fight for black civil rights.

Hungry in Mississippi

James's mother, Octavia Allen, had moved to Chicago to escape southern racism and the grinding poverty her family lived in.

James Forman grew up on a farm like this one near Clarksdale, Mississippi. He plowed fields of cotton, corn, and other crops.

She had trouble supporting her son because she had not married his father. When James was eleven months old, Octavia sent him to live with her mother in Mississippi because she thought he would be better off there.

Jane Allen, who James affectionately called "Mama Jane," was a widow; her husband, Edmond, had died during a widespread outbreak of influenza during World War I. The 180-acre farm (73ha) she shared with family members was located about 30 miles (48km) from Clarksdale, Mississippi. Forman lived in his grandmother's four-room house, which was heated by a wood stove and lacked indoor plumbing. The family did not even have an outhouse, the crude outdoor toilet most rural people used during this period. James and other family members had their bowel movements in an orchard to fertilize its apple and peach trees, an agricultural method used in many countries for thousands of years. The family had a mule to plow fields in which they planted cotton, corn, and other crops.

Forman was almost always hungry as a child because the family was very poor. Most blacks in the South during this period were poor because of racist laws and policies that denied them a quality education and racist attitudes that blocked their opportunities to obtain good jobs even if they were educated. Compounding that institutionalized poverty was the Great Depression, which began in 1929 and crippled the national economy for more than a decade. Forman once explained in an interview that family members sometimes begged for food because they were on the edge of starvation. "We used to go to people's houses and [ask for food]. We were very hungry, extremely hungry. In fact we were so hungry that, there was a bank [small hill] on the side of the road that was supposed to have some vitamins to it. And we would take this dirt and try to eat it in order to try and get some [nourishment]."[7]

Eating dirt or clay was something both poor southern whites and blacks did to alleviate severe hunger.

Despite the grinding poverty, the young boy was relatively happy. He delighted in reading, something he learned to do at a young age from his aunt Thelma, a schoolteacher who taught him at home. His grandmother also tried to educate him in simple ways, like making him spell the names of the different types of food she gave him to eat.

Forman's mother sometimes visited and took her son back to Chicago for short periods. Eventually, however, life was so difficult in the rural areas that his grandmother realized James would be better off in Chicago. She told him, "Well, spote [the way she pronounced his nickname 'sport'], write to your mother and tell her to come to get you because I've done what I could for you."[8] So at age six, Forman moved back to Chicago.

Growing Up in Chicago

In Chicago, James lived in a four-room apartment with his mother and stepfather and went to school on a regular basis for the first time. In 1932 Octavia had married James "Pops" Rufus, who owned a gas station. James believed Rufus was his real father until he was fourteen years old when he accidentally found his birth certificate and discovered that his biological father was Jackson Forman. James later met Forman, who was a cab driver. Even though James never became close to his biological father,

Jim Crow

Jim Crow was the racist system of state and local laws that denied southern blacks many of their civil rights for nearly a century. The name Jim Crow, a mocking term for blacks, arose from the stage act of Thomas Dartmouth Rice, a white entertainer in the nineteenth century. Rice, like many whites in that era, would blacken his face and perform racist parodies of African Americans in songs and comedy skits. The derisive name became more sinister in the late nineteenth century when racist southerners passed laws that denied blacks many of their constitutional rights and created a segregated society. Jim Crow laws passed by state and local governments banned blacks from many public places reserved for whites, such as restaurants, hotels, and movie theaters. Blacks also had to sit separately from whites on trains and buses and use different public bathrooms and drinking fountains. This segregation, which was illegal under the U.S. Constitution, extended to schools, libraries, swimming pools, and other public facilities operated by local governments even though blacks paid taxes that funded them. Many state laws made it hard, if not impossible, for blacks to register to vote, which enabled whites to control them politically. James Forman experienced that racism as a child in Mississippi. It was to stop such mistreatment of blacks that he joined the Student Nonviolent Coordinating Committee as an adult.

An African American enters a Missouri movie theater at the back "colored" entrance. Jim Crow laws passed by state and local governments banned blacks from many public places reserved for whites and created segregated schools, libraries, swimming pools, and even public restrooms and drinking fountains.

he changed his last name to Forman when he was eighteen years old, after years of having the name James Rufus.

James began his formal education at age seven at St. Anselm's School, a Roman Catholic institution with just one white student. Several years later he began attending Betsy Ross Grammar School because his family had trouble paying tuition at the private school. James never had toys or a bicycle, but one Christmas he did get a wagon. His mother told him the present was from Santa Claus, but James, a smart young boy, knew that was not true because he had heard his parents putting the wagon together the night before.

To make money, James saved newspapers and sold them to junkyards. He also stole milk bottles and turned them in at stores for the penny deposit. The seven-year-old also began selling the *Chicago Defender*, a respected black newspaper. James avidly read stories and articles in the newspaper, many of which were about the violence southern whites used to control blacks. In his autobiography, *The Making of Black Revolutionaries*, Forman wrote that the stories had angered him and had made him want to do something to help his fellow African Americans. "Each week the paper would contain the story of a new horror perpetrated against the race. I wanted to do something about these injustices, the lynching here and beatings there, the discrimination everywhere. I vowed over and over that someday I would help to end this treatment [of] my people."[9]

The *Defender* featured articles by black leaders like W.E.B. DuBois and Booker T. Washington that shaped the young boy's thinking about what it meant to be black in a nation controlled by whites. James was especially drawn to the philosophy of Du-Bois, a founder of the National Association for the Advancement of Colored People (NAACP). DuBois was the first black to earn a doctorate from Harvard University. He believed blacks could accomplish anything if they were educated. Forman decided he would go to college, but when he entered Chicago's Englewood High School his decision to seek a higher education created a conflict with his mother over his choice of courses. In an interview, Forman explained the situation:

"My mother is a very beautiful person and she encouraged me always to make decisions for myself. But on this particular issue

CHICAGO
DEFENORR
PHOTO.

CHICAGO DEFENDER BOOTH
AT THE CHICAGO DEFENDER COOKING SCHOOL.
SAVOY BALLROOM, OCT. 27-28-29-1932.

At the age of seven James Forman began selling the *Chicago Defender*, a respected black newspaper.

of what I should study in high school, she objected to what I wanted to do. I wanted to take college preparatory courses [but] she said 'You've got to be able to get a job.'"[10]

Forman's mother thought her son should take industrial arts classes because she was worried that discrimination would make it difficult for a black man with a college degree to find work. He understood her fears but was determined to go to college anyway. In 1947 Forman graduated with honors from high school and began attending Wilson Junior College in Chicago, but his education would soon be interrupted.

Military Life

While attending college, Forman was not able to earn enough money to support himself even though he continued working at his stepfather's gas station. So after just one semester, Forman enlisted in the U.S. Air Force. When the eighteen-year-old signed his induction papers, he used the name Forman for the first time. Forman originally enlisted for three years, but his service was extended for one year when the Korean War began in 1950.

Military life was disillusioning for Forman because units were segregated, and blacks were not treated equally with whites. Although black enlistees had been promised the opportunity for technical training, they were almost always limited to schooling for menial jobs as cooks, bakers, and mechanics. That angered Forman even though he had qualified for advanced training and was given a desk job in which he classified soldiers for different military careers. Forman later wrote that he hated his military service because as a soldier he was "supposedly protecting a system of government which I had grown to hate"[11] because of how it treated blacks. He also came to believe that the military was "a dehumanizing machine which destroys thought and creativity."[12]

Forman was discharged from the service on September 23, 1951. He moved to Los Angeles, where he married a woman named Mary, whom he had known before, and enrolled in the University of California. One night in 1953, when Forman left the university library where he had been studying for hours, two white policemen arrested him because he resembled the description of someone who had committed a robbery. They took Forman to the police station and began questioning him about the robbery. The interrogations continued off-and-on for three days. During that time, policemen beat him and taunted him with racial slurs while trying to make him admit he had committed the crime. Police brutality against blacks was common in that era. It was an especially frightening and degrading experience for Forman because the police refused to check his claim of innocence by contacting people who could prove he had been studying at the library at the time of the robbery.

Forman was finally released without being charged, but the experience left him exhausted physically, mentally, and emotionally. The brutal brush with racism led to a mental breakdown,

A Young Boy's Introduction to Racism

———————◼———————

James Forman learned as a child that many white people believed blacks to be inferior. In his autobiography, *The Making of Black Revolutionaries*, Forman described an incident in Memphis, Tennessee, in which a white man refused to let him sit at the counter in a store and drink a soda he had paid for. Because of segregation, blacks could buy soda but they could not sit at the counter reserved for whites or drink their soda from a glass like white customers could. Forman describes the conversation he had with the racist storeowner:

"You have to drink your Coke back here. You can't sit on those stools."

"But ... why?" [I] could not understand what right he had to tell me where I had to drink my Coke, why I couldn't sit on the stool.

"Boy, you're a n****r," he said in a flat voice.

"A what?" I asked [because] I didn't really understand the word.

"A n****r, and Negroes don't sit on the stools here."

I put the Coke down [and] left the drugstore, sobbing.

James Forman. *The Making of Black Revolutionaries*. Seattle: University of Washington Press, 1997, p. 19.

and he was admitted to the Veterans Neuropsychiatric Hospital in Los Angeles. In "Driven Insane," the title of the first chapter of his autobiography, Forman describes his descent into madness: "Nerves are crossed . . . twisted . . . tossed . . . all in a maze. . . . Cops won this round. . . . Racism . . . rooted deep. . . . American culture no exit . . . no way out. Nerves gone. . . . Alone. . . . Sleep. . . . Insane! No lights . . . no shiny lights. . . . Alone . . . deep sleep . . . sleep. . . . Lights out . . . dark . . . deep . . . sleep . . . cool . . . calm . . . coma."[13]

While Forman was being treated in the hospital, his wife, Mary, visited him even though they had been separated at the time of his arrest. The love she showed him helped Forman recover. They reunited after Forman was released from the hospital, but they were not happy together and decided to divorce. In March 1954 Forman returned to Chicago to resume his college studies.

Fighting for Civil Rights

At Chicago's Roosevelt University, Forman became a leader in student government and graduated in 1957 with a bachelor of arts degree in public administration. Forman's grades were so good that he received a grant to attend Boston University to do graduate work in African Research and Studies.

James Forman began working as a public school teacher in Chicago, but in the fall of 1960 he became involved in the civil rights movement. Here he speaks at a church urging the congregation to demand equal rights.

Like many blacks during this period, Forman had become excited about the fight for civil rights that was being led by Rev. Martin Luther King Jr. and others. Beginning in 1955, King had led a boycott of the Montgomery, Alabama, bus system to end segregated bus seating. It was a major victory for blacks when the U.S. Supreme Court, responding to a lawsuit filed by protesters, ruled that Alabama's laws requiring segregated seating on buses were unconstitutional.

King's heroic stand renewed Forman's interest in fighting for black civil rights. In 1958 he abandoned his graduate studies to go to Little Rock, Arkansas, as a reporter for the *Chicago Defender*. Little Rock schools were being integrated after courts had ordered the city to obey the historic 1954 *Brown v. Board of Education* Supreme Court decision that prohibited segregated schools. Forman wrote several stories about the desegregation efforts, including descriptions of the violence that whites had used in their attempts to prevent it.

Forman then returned to Chicago to take classes at Chicago Teachers College. He began working as a public school teacher, but in the fall of 1960, his interest in civil rights led him to go to Fayette County, Tennessee. There, some seven hundred black families had been evicted from their homes by their white employers, who owned the houses the families lived in. The employers had evicted the families because they had tried to register to vote. The evicted blacks were living in a makeshift tent city and struggling to survive because local white merchants refused to sell them necessities such as food and gasoline. The Congress of Racial Equality (CORE), a civil rights organization that pioneered the use of nonviolent direct action, such as sit-ins and boycotts, asked Forman to help its Emergency Relief Committee, which was providing food, clothing, and other aid to Fayette County blacks.

In addition to writing stories about the plight of the evicted workers for the *Chicago Defender*, Forman also wrote other articles to publicize the injustice being done in Fayette County. In gathering facts for his stories, Forman interviewed many Fayette County blacks. On Christmas night 1960, in the tent she was living in, Georgia Mae Turner told Forman why she had risked her home to be able to vote: "They say if you register, you going to

James Forman, right, gives instructions in Albany, Georgia, on how a nonviolent protester should respond when confronted by law enforcement while demonstrating against segregation.

have a hard time. Well, I had a hard time before I registered. Hard times—you could have named me 'Georgia Mae Hard Times.' The reason I registered, because I want to be a citizen. I registered so that my children could get their freedom."[14]

It took two years for the federal government to stop the evictions and economic warfare against people who simply wanted to vote, a right that was not protected for many southern blacks until passage of the Voting Rights Act of 1965.

James Forman's Mission in Life

In 1964 acclaimed novelist and poet Robert Penn Warren interviewed James Forman and other civil rights leaders for his book *Who Speaks for the Negro?* Warren noted that before Forman became executive secretary of the Student Nonviolent Coordinating Committee, he had been in the air force, gone to college, and worked as a reporter and schoolteacher. Forman told him that even though he had done many things in his life, they had all been motivated by the personal goal he had had since he was a child:

> Well, it was all up for grabs, you know. Really, I have never been able to clearly state at any one point in my life that I'm going to be this or I'm going to be that. Or that this is what I want to do. I've been very ambivalent about many things, you know, and the ambivalence revolved I think basically around the whole question of whatever it is that I do, how can this best integrate with the conception of doing something for the Negro in the United States.

Quoted in Robert Penn Warren. *Who Speaks for the Negro?*, an archival collection. Interview with James Forman, 1964. Tape 1. Original Transcript. http://whospeaks.library.vanderbilt.edu/sites/default/files/Pg.%20969-984%20Reel%201%20James%20Forman%20Interview%2C%20Tape%201.pdf.

Back and Forth

Although the Fayette County situation deepened Forman's resolve to stop racist discrimination, he returned to teaching in early 1961 to support himself. He was torn, however, about leaving the South because he believed it was time for blacks to stand up and fight for their rights. He would follow news of the growing civil rights movement with the strong belief that someday he would return and join it.

Chapter Two

Sit-ins and SNCC

One of the demeaning effects of Jim Crow was that blacks could buy things in stores but could not purchase and eat food at the stores' lunch counters, which in that era were the most popular places to have inexpensive meals. But on February 1, 1960, four North Carolina Agricultural and Technical College students in Greensboro, North Carolina, sat down at a Woolworth's lunch counter in a direct challenge to the racist policy. When Ezell Blair Jr., Franklin McCain, Joseph McNeil, and David Richmond politely asked for cups of coffee, a white waitress told them: "We don't serve colored in here."[15] Instead of leaving in shame, they stayed until closing, refusing to be denied service because of the color of their skin. And because the four young men believed it was time for blacks to stand up for their rights, they returned the next day with sixteen more students to start a bold new phase in the battle for civil rights. Blair told a reporter covering the sit-ins: "Negro adults have been complacent and fearful. . . . It is time for someone to wake up and change the situation . . . and we decided to start here."[16] Blacks had used sit-ins in the past without any results. This time their bravery inspired so many other young people to adopt the tactic that the protests became powerful enough to make a difference.

By the end of February, students and young activists were staging similar protests in more than thirty communities in seven states, and by the end of April there had been sit-ins in every

Demonstrators protest outside the Greensboro, North Carolina, Woolworth's store in February 1960. They urged a boycott of Woolworth's stores until segregation ended.

southern state. The sit-ins delighted veteran civil rights activist Ella Baker, who describes how word of the exciting new crusade against racism spread like wildfire among blacks: "A sister to a brother, members of the same fraternity, girlfriend to boyfriend, or simply calling up contacts, friends asking 'What is happening on your campus?'"[17]

The first sit-ins were peaceful. But as they continued, white racists began to fear the sit-ins might succeed in toppling Jim Crow and began to strike back, and the protests became dangerous to participate in.

The Sit-ins Spread

The demonstrations, which some people at first called "sit-downs," spread rapidly because a younger generation of black college students was no longer content with the racist status quo that they felt their elders had too benignly accepted. In Atlanta, a statement by students from several schools who had joined together to stage protests explained why they were determined to fight for their rights no matter what the cost: "Every normal human being wants to walk the earth with dignity and abhors any and all [restrictions] placed upon him because of race or color. In essence, this is the meaning of the sit-down protests that are sweeping the nation today."[18]

On February 13, less than two weeks after the first Greensboro sit-in, 124 students from several universities in Nashville, Tennessee, including white supporters, went to three downtown lunch counters and were refused service. The protesters included Diane Nash, John Lewis, and Julian Bond, who would all become important SNCC leaders. Although the number of protesters grew to more than three hundred during sit-ins on February 18 and February 20, they initially met with little resistance from whites. In fact, Nash remembers that the protests seemed to frighten white employees in the targeted stores: "The first sit-in we had was really funny, because the waitresses were nervous. They must have dropped two thousand dollars worth of dishes that day."[19]

But on February 27, the sit-ins turned violent. Angry whites entered Nashville stores and began shouting racial slurs and attacking students who were peacefully sitting at lunch counters. Angeline Butler remembers the ugly scene at a McClelland's five-and-dime (a variety store where most items cost a nickel or a dime): "We faced almost instant violence as the store filled up with shoppers and spectators. They threw things at us, yelled insulting remarks, and put burning cigarettes down our backs. Paul LaPrad, a white transfer student to Fisk [University] from De-Pauw University, was badly beaten by two young white men."[20]

White policemen who responded to the incidents arrested eighty-one protesters on charges of loitering and disorderly conduct but none of the whites who had attacked them. Protesters did not strike back or resist white civilians who beat them or white policemen who brutally took them to jail because James Lawson, a thirty-two-year-old Vanderbilt University divinity student, had trained them to act nonviolently in such situations.

Two weeks after the Greensboro sit-ins began, eight black Florida Agricultural and Mechanical University (FAMU) students

James Lawson

■

James Lawson believed in nonviolence so strongly that he went to jail to uphold that principle. During the Korean War in 1951, Lawson declared himself a conscientious objector to war and refused to register for the military draft. A Methodist minister, he could have obtained a deferment as a student or a minister. Instead, he protested war by serving eighteen months in prison for refusing to register. While attending Vanderbilt University in Nashville, Tennessee, Lawson introduced students to the tactic of nonviolent protest, which became the founding principle of the Student Nonviolent Coordinating Committee. Lawson once explained that his commitment to nonviolence stemmed from his religious beliefs:

> When you are a child of God you try thereby to imitate Jesus, in the midst of evil. Which means, if someone slaps you on one cheek, you turn the other cheek, which is an act of resistance. It means that you do not only love your neighbor, but you recognize that even the enemy has a spark of God in them [and] needs to be treated as you, yourself, want to be treated.

Public Broadcasting Service. "This Far by Faith: Witnesses to Faith." www.pbs.org/thisfarbyfaith/witnesses/james_lawson.html.

James Lawson is arrested for demonstrating against segregation.

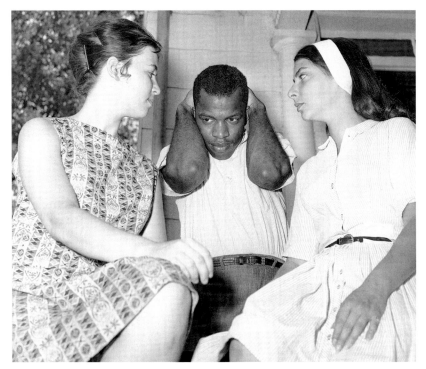

John Lewis explains self-protective measures to two white students participating in a civil rights seminar sponsored by SNCC.

sat down at a Woolworth's lunch counter in Tallahassee, Florida. Their first few protests were uneventful. But on March 12 police arrested almost 250 people when black FAMU and white Florida State University students who supported them took their places at Woolworth's and McCrory's lunch counters. When nearly one thousand people marched to protest the arrests, police used tear-gas to disrupt the demonstration. Patricia Stephens suffered an eye injury when police sprayed tear gas directly into her face, temporarily blinding her: "I couldn't see, but I could hear the screams of the students,"[21] she recalls. Permanent damage from the gas forced Stephens to wear dark glasses the rest of her life whenever she was in bright light.

Neither arrests nor violence could stop the powerful new movement to overturn Jim Crow. Baker, a fifty-six-year-old civil rights veteran, believed that students spread across the South needed to meet so they could more effectively plan their powerful protests. Baker was director of the Southern Christian Leadership

Conference (SCLC), a civil rights organization founded after the Montgomery bus boycott by a group of black ministers dedicated to fighting racism, of which Rev. Martin Luther King Jr. was president. Baker convinced the SCLC to put up $800 to fund a meeting of students at Shaw University in Raleigh, North Carolina.

Baker had wanted students to decide the future course of their fight against racism. Instead, they created SNCC.

SNCC Is Born

From April 15 to 17, 1960, which was Easter weekend, more than three hundred students from fifty-eight sit-in centers in twelve states as well as students from nineteen northern colleges came together in Raleigh to discuss southern racism. Although King was one of several people who addressed the young protesters, the most powerful speech was given by Lawson, who like many other students had been expelled from school for taking part in the protests. Lawson believed that older civil rights groups had relied too heavily on court decisions to achieve racial justice and that more nonviolent protests were necessary to help blacks achieve equality. Lawson exhorted the students to keep fighting hard for racial justice: "Get moving! The pace of social change is too slow. At this rate it will be at least another generation before the major forms of segregation disappear [and] before the American negro attains first-class citizenship. Most of us will be grandparents before we can live normal lives."[22]

King had hoped the students would become a youth wing of the SCLC. Baker, however, advised student leaders to form their own group so they could retain control of their activities and be independent from other civil rights organizations. After two days of discussion, the students created a temporary committee whose fifteen members agreed to meet May 13–14 in Atlanta. In this first official meeting, the group formalized plans for a new organization, which they named the Student Nonviolent Coordinating Committee. They elected Marion Barry, a student at Fisk University in Nashville, as SNCC's first chairman and named Baker a senior adviser. They also approved a lofty statement of purpose that dedicated SNCC to nonviolence as the best way to win support for their cause of racial justice: "We affirm the philosophical or

Diane Nash

Diane Nash was a twenty-two-year-old college student at Fisk University in Nashville, Tennessee, when she joined the sit-in movement and helped found the Student Nonviolent Coordinating Committee. Nash had grown up in Chicago, and her exposure to southern racism in college made her determined to fight it. In an interview, Nash once explained that it was humiliating for blacks who purchased food downtown to have to sit outside on the curb or in an alley to eat their purchase instead of sitting down inside like whites did. She also explained how hard it was to protest and go to school at the same time:

> It was hard. One way we did it was just by working long hours. A lot of people had 8 A.M. classes. Our meetings were usually in the evening, after dinner. But we had so much work to do that frequently we would have 6 A.M. meetings. Then during the day we'd go to class, do our schoolwork, and the assignments we had taken on in the meetings. Sometimes there'd be sit-ins or demonstrations during the day. So our schedule was tight.

Quoted in Judy Richardson. "An Interview with Diane Nash." *Footsteps*, May–June 2000, p. 24.

Diane Nash, shown here in 2011, was a college student when she helped found the Student Nonviolent Coordinating Committee.

religious ideal of nonviolence as the foundation of our purpose, the presupposition of our belief, and the manner of our action. [Through] nonviolence, courage displaces fear. Love transcends hate. Acceptance dissipates prejudice; hope ends despair. Faith reconciles doubt. Peace dominates war. Mutual regards cancel enmity. Justice for all overthrows injustice."[23]

SNCC established its headquarters in Atlanta, first in office space that the SCLC had provided and later in a nearby building. The new organization hired Jane Stembridge, a white student from Virginia who was studying at Union Theological Seminary in New York, as its secretary. Baker helped the group begin raising funds, and the first donation, of one hundred dollars, came from former First Lady Eleanor Roosevelt. SNCC needed funding so it could stay in contact with students returning to school in the fall and help them continue their protests.

A Victory in Nashville

After the Easter meeting in Raleigh, there were more sit-ins and protests than ever before. And eventually, they began changing the culture of racism that gripped the South. Two days after college students in Raleigh had dedicated themselves to nonviolence to end Jim Crow, racist whites in Nashville used violence to uphold it. On April 19, a bomb destroyed the home of Z. Alexander Looby, a sit-in supporter who was the only black member of the Nashville City Council. Although neither Looby nor his wife was harmed, 2,500 blacks marched on city hall to protest the bombing. When mayor Ben West talked with the protesters, Nash boldly asked him if, as a man and not as an elected official, he believed segregation was morally right. To the protesters' surprise, West said he did not. He also agreed to help them desegregate lunch counters. Years later, Nash said that West's honest answer was a key to winning the battle to end such discrimination: "I have a lot of respect for the way he responded. He didn't have to respond the way he did. He said that he felt like it was wrong for citizens of Nashville to be discriminated against at the lunch counter solely on the basis of the color of their skin. And I think that was the turning point."[24]

Only a few weeks later, on May 10, six Nashville businesses opened their lunch counters to blacks. It was not only the sit-ins and West that were responsible for the victory, however. While the sit-ins were going on, blacks and their white supporters had refused to buy anything from segregated stores. This financial boycott hurt the storeowners' businesses and was important in forcing them to agree to desegregation. By August 1961, restaurants in 119 southern cities had agreed to serve blacks. The victories were the result of protests by more than seventy thousand people, most of them black, of whom 3,600 were arrested and hundreds beaten.

However, various forms of discrimination continued for many years in most southern areas because racist whites refused to give in to black demands. Civil rights protesters in the South soon began targeting other aspects of Jim Crow.

Black students confront Nashville police during demonstrations against segregation in that city. The students made an unexpected ally in Nashville mayor Ben West, who backed desegregation.

Other Protests

In Biloxi, Mississippi, the twenty-six miles of beach along the Gulf of Mexico was segregated, with whites reserving the best spots for themselves. On April 14, 1960, a group of 126 blacks went to a beach that had been designated for whites only in what they called a "wade-in." At first there was no violence, but on the third wade-in protest on April 24, forty whites wielding chains, tire irons, and other weapons attacked the demonstrators. One of the demonstrators, James Black, recalls: "I saw [Wilmer B.] McDaniel beaten to within an inch of his life. He fell, and was hit with chains, and the sand became bloody."[25] Afterward Dr. Gilbert Mason, who had organized the protests, tended to the wounded. While Mason was treating victims, a white policeman threatened him with a gun and ordered him to get off the beach. That night, whites in cars roared through black neighborhoods, threatening people and firing guns.

Jail-No-Bail

One of the most effective protest tactics in the 1960s was "jail-no-bail," in which people who were arrested stayed in jail instead of paying a fine or putting up bail. The Student Nonviolent Coordinating Committee (SNCC) pioneered this tactic on February 1, 1961, after nine men were convicted of trespassing at a sit-in at a McCrory's lunch counter in Rock Hill, South Carolina. They refused to pay a $100-fine and instead served thirty days of hard labor at the York County Prison Farm. In 2007 Thomas Gaither, one of the men who became known as the Friendship Nine, said they did it because "we thought it was time to raise the level of commitment to show how serious we were about trying to transform our society into a more just society." Staying in jail strengthened Rock Hill protests by showing people how dedicated the protesters were. However, it was also a practical move by SNCC to avoid paying the fines because it did not have enough money to pay bail for all the people being arrested in similar protests.

Quoted in PBS *News Hour*. "'Jail, No Bail' Idea Stymied Cities' Profiting from Civil Rights Protesters," March 7, 2011. www.pbs.org/newshour/bb/social_issues/jan-june11/jail_03-07.html.

In Durham, North Carolina, blacks who had staged lunch counter sit-ins in 1960 turned their attention in January 1961 to the downtown theater reserved for whites. In a unique protest that made it hard for the theater to operate, blacks waited in line to buy tickets; when they were refused a ticket they simply got back in line, which made it hard for whites to buy tickets. White supporters also bought tickets and handed them to blacks, which created more problems when they tried to enter the segregated theater. The protest continued for months even though it was often cold and rainy. In a 2003 interview, protester Fay Bryant Mahyo recalled that she and the other protesters were willing to endure such discomfort because they believed in what they were doing: "You just sort of grew strong as you marched—you were angry, and I guess that was where you were really getting your strength from, your inner anger as you walked around the Carolina Theater in the rain . . . as you listened to people calling you names and spitting at you and everything."[26]

In Jackson, Mississippi, the Jackson Municipal Library barred blacks. On March 27, 1961, nine students from Tougaloo College entered the library to study. When they sat down, the librarian called the police, and the students were arrested. Joyce Ladner, one of four female protesters, explains why they chose the library for a protest: "Mississippi at the time was considered to be too racist and violent for lunch-counter sit-ins, so the library sit-in was chosen by Medgar Evers and others because it was supported by taxpayers, both black and white."[27] Two years later Evers, a civil rights leader in Mississippi, was shot to death in the driveway of his home. He was wearing a "Jim Crow Must Go" T-shirt when he was murdered.

"Bigger than a Hamburger"

With a budget of only $3,100 in 1960 and only a few staff members, SNCC was not able to accomplish very much in the first six months of its existence. However, the young people who created SNCC added new strength to the fight for civil rights and established their organization as one that racist whites would have to contend with in the future. Some older black leaders disagreed with SNCC's aggressive tactics in challenging Jim Crow and refused to believe the young upstarts would ever achieve their goals. Baker was not one of them. She knew the young people were willing to sacrifice themselves to end racism. In June 1960, Baker wrote an article about what SNCC hoped to accomplish: "The student leadership conference made it crystal clear that the current sit-ins and demonstrations are concerned with something much bigger than a hamburger or even a giant-sized Coke. Whatever may be the difference in approach to their goal, the Negro and white students, North and South, are seeking to rid America of the scourge of racial segregation and discrimination—not only at lunch counters, but in every aspect of life."[28]

In the next few years, SNCC would topple Jim Crow and help blacks win their most important civil rights.

Chapter Three

Freedom Riders and James Forman

Sit-in successes inspired the Congress of Racial Equality in 1961 to partner with SNCC to resurrect a civil rights tactic that CORE had first tried fifteen years earlier. On April 9, 1947, eight white and eight black men had begun a two-week trip that became known as the Journey of Reconciliation through southern states to desegregate interstate bus travel. Whites and blacks were arrested several times for disobeying segregated seating on buses. Their purpose was to challenge the Jim Crow state laws and policies that required blacks to sit in the back of the bus despite earlier Supreme Court rulings that had banned segregation in interstate bus travel. In North Carolina, riders were sentenced to jail terms that forced them to do hard labor for up to ninety days. The 1947 ride garnered national publicity but failed to stop the discriminatory practice.

In 1961, following the earlier example, seven whites and six blacks, including John Lewis and Hank Thomas of SNCC, decided to ride the bus through Virginia, North and South Carolina, Georgia, Alabama, and Mississippi en route to New Orleans for a civil rights rally on May 17. On May 4, 1961, the self-dubbed Freedom Riders split into two groups to board Greyhound and Trailways buses in Washington, D.C., where Jim Crow had been outlawed. The riders sat together near the

An Alabama fireman hoses down a bus used by Freedom Riders to protest segregation on interstate buses. The bus was burnt by segregationist whites who also beat the riders.

front of the buses and during stops at bus stations the black riders attempted to use white restrooms and eating places. For ten days the rides continued despite the arrests of some riders and several violent incidents, including one in Rock Hill, South Carolina, in which future SNCC chairman Lewis was beaten for entering the white waiting room.

On May 14, white mobs, that included members of the white supremacist group Ku Klux Klan (KKK), attacked riders at bus stations in Anniston and Birmingham, Alabama. So many riders were severely injured that CORE leaders decided to stop the rides. But thanks to Diane Nash, the rides continued.

SNCC Steps In

Nash was in Nashville, Tennessee, when she heard that CORE was going to end the rides. In addition to being a SNCC founder, Nash headed the Nashville Student Movement. Even though she knew riders would be in danger, she called Southern Christian Leadership Conference head Fred Shuttlesworth and said she would recruit students to replace the injured riders. Shuttlesworth, who had been arrested for trying to rescue riders from the Birmingham mob, tried to dissuade Nash, warning her: "Young lady, do you know that the Freedom Riders were almost killed here?"[29] Nash ignored his advice because she believed the rides had to continue to show that blacks would not surrender to white violence. "The impression would have been that whenever a movement starts, all you have to do is attack it with massive violence and the blacks will stop,"[30] she commented.

On the morning of May 20, sixteen black and three white college students left Birmingham to continue the ride. Alabama Highway Patrol cars escorted the bus for protection, but when it reached the Montgomery city limits the cars suddenly disappeared. When the bus arrived at the terminal, it was surrounded by hundreds of whites shouting racial slurs and wielding baseball bats, lead pipes, and chains. Montgomery police officers who were supposed to be there to protect riders had mysteriously left the area just minutes earlier. As riders stepped off the bus, whites attacked them. Lewis, William Barbee, and Jim Zwerg, a white from Appleton, Wisconsin, studying at Fisk University in Nashville, were all beaten unconscious. Police did not arrive until more than an hour later.

The vicious beatings, one of the most brutal incidents in the new fight for civil rights, shocked the nation, but it did not stop the Freedom Riders. Interviewed in their separate rooms in a segregated hospital, Barbee told reporters, "As soon as we've recovered from this, we'll start again," and Zwerg agreed, saying, "We are prepared to die."[31] Four days later, on May 24, two more busloads of Freedom Riders left Montgomery for Jackson, Mississippi. When they arrived there, they were arrested for trying to desegregate public restroom and dining facilities.

The threat of arrest also failed to deter the Freedom Riders. More volunteers continued the rides throughout the summer and kept getting arrested in Jackson. Under the "jail-no-bail" tactic, in which the arrestees refused to pay bail or fines for their release, riders began to fill Mississippi jails to overflowing. Crowding got so bad that some were even sent to Parchman Penitentiary, a southern prison notorious for its brutal treatment of blacks. At

John Lewis Is Beaten

John Lewis, one of the thirteen original Freedom Riders, became chairman of the Student Nonviolent Coordinating Committee (SNCC) in 1963. Lewis, who in 1986 was elected a U.S. representative from Georgia, was one of the most heroic civil rights leaders in the 1960s. He was beaten unconscious on May 20, 1961, as he and other Freedom Riders got off a bus in Montgomery, Alabama. He recalls:

> [When] we arrived at the bus station, it was eerie. Just a strange feeling. It was so quiet, so peaceful, nothing. And the moment we started down the steps of that bus, there was an angry mob. [The] mob turned on the members of the press [and] they beat up all of the reporters, then they turned on the black male members and white male members of the group. I was beaten—I think I was hit with a sort of crate thing that holds soda bottles—and left lying unconscious there in the streets of Montgomery.

Quoted in Henry Hampton and Steve Fayer. *Voices of Freedom: An Oral History of the Civil Rights Movement from the 1950s Through the 1980s.* New York: Bantam Books, 1990, pp. 86–87.

John Lewis is arrested in Montgomery, Alabama, after being beaten by an angry mob when the Freedom Rider bus he was on arrived at the Montgomery bus station.

An angry mob of whites blocks a Freedom Rider bus from leaving. Mobs of whites slashed tires, burned buses, and beat riders all along the Freedom Ride route.

Parchman, guards beat some of the riders and used electric cattle prods to punish them for singing protest songs. Future SNCC chairman Stokley Carmichael recalls: "When [the prod] touched your skin, the pain was sharp and excruciating, at once a jolting shock and a burn. You could actually see (puffs of smoke) and smell (the odor of roasting flesh) your skin burning."[32]

The mounting media coverage and public outrage over treatment of the riders finally forced the federal government to act. President John F. Kennedy ordered the Interstate Commerce Commission to issue a new rule enforcing the desegregation of interstate bus travel. It went into effect on November 1, 1961. SNCC's involvement in the rides gave the group a huge boost in prestige among other civil rights groups. But it would take James Forman to help SNCC reach its full potential in fighting for black rights.

Forman Joins SNCC

The Freedom Rides had excited Forman's imagination so much that in the summer of 1961 he went to Nashville. There, he participated in a protest at a supermarket to force the owner to hire more blacks and met SNCC members Nash and Paul Brooks, one of the second group of Freedom Riders. Forman discussed with them a novel he had been writing about a group of young people, both black and white, who were committed to fighting Jim Crow. Forman had begun the book in 1958 after reporting on school desegregation in Little Rock, Arkansas; he finished the novel, but it was never published.

Forman returned to teaching in Chicago but in September Brooks called and asked him to consider becoming SNCC's executive secretary. SNCC members like Nash and Brooks had realized SNCC needed someone to direct and coordinate their activities in various cities and handle organizational chores like hiring workers, raising funds, and publicizing the group. They chose Forman because when they met him, he had impressed them with the ideas he had described from his novel about how to manage a civil rights group.

Despite Forman's passion for fighting for black rights, he did not know at first how to respond to the offer. He told Brooks: "'Well,' I said, 'Man just wait a minute now. This requires a slight degree of thought. You don't just say, am I willing to leave my job and so forth just like that.'"[33] In addition to leaving his teaching job, Forman also had to consider how moving to Atlanta to head SNCC would affect his wife, Mildred, whom he had married in 1959. But after Nash and other SNCC members came to Chicago and met with Forman and his wife, they both agreed to join SNCC.

Forman's salary to manage SNCC would be just sixty dollars a week. The group believed its workers should receive only subsistence wages so they would better be able to relate to the people they were helping, who were mostly poor. Still, Forman's salary was nearly six times the standard pay of ten dollars a week for field secretaries, who went to various cities to conduct civil rights campaigns.

When Forman flew to Atlanta, he was disillusioned at his first sight of the office he would work in to oversee SNCC's civil rights work. The small room with dirty walls had mail all over the floor and desks littered with papers that he knew nothing about. The telephone was ringing constantly with questions from reporters wanting facts about a protest by high school students in McComb, Mississippi, where SNCC was trying to register voters. He answered the calls but said he could not release any information at the moment; he had to give that answer because he knew nothing about the protest. Forman later wrote that his introduction to his new job was difficult and disheartening. "I began to realize what was really in store for me. [Was] there anyone to answer the phone if I went out? What was my assignment, what was I supposed to be doing? I thought of orienting myself somewhat by

Parchman Penitentiary

William Mahoney was a student at Howard University, an all-black school in Washington, D.C., who volunteered to continue the Freedom Rides after the violence in Montgomery, Alabama. On May 28, Mahoney and other Freedom Riders were arrested in Jackson, Mississippi, on a charge of breach of the peace. Mahoney and fellow Freedom Riders were first imprisoned in a county jail and later in Parchman Penitentiary. Mahoney describes what prison was like:

> The thirty or more of us occupied five cells and a dining hall on the top floor. At night we slept on lumpy bags of cotton and were locked in a small, dirty, blood-spattered, roach-infested cell. Days were passed in the hot, overcrowded dining room playing cards, reading, praying, and, as was almost inevitable, fighting among ourselves over the most petty things. Time crawled painfully, 15 days becoming 45 meals, 360 hours, 100 card games or 3 letters from home. [But] morale remained high; insults and brutality became the subject of jokes and skits. The jailers, initially hostile, were broken down by our responding to them with respect and with good humor.

Quoted in Juan Williams. *Eyes on the Prize: America's Civil Rights Years, 1954–1965.* New York: Viking Penguin, 1987, p. 126.

James Forman, right, speaks at a press conference as director of the Student Nonviolent Coordinating Committee. By the spring of 1963 Forman had transformed SNCC from a loose coalition into a political force for blacks' civil rights.

looking through the files. What files? There weren't any to speak of. Utter chaos."[34]

Forman, however, was the perfect person to bring order to SNCC and change chaos into coordinated, effective action that would help blacks finally win their civil rights.

Taking Charge of SNCC

When Forman took over SNCC in 1961, it was a loose-knit coalition of college students who protested part-time. By the spring of 1963, he had transformed it into a dynamic cadre of 180 full-time workers, most of them students who had graduated or quit school to focus full-time on the fight for civil rights. Forman's personnel experience in the air force was essential to helping him choose the right people to conduct SNCC projects and staff its Atlanta office. Dorothy "Dottie" Miller, a white college graduate from New York, was one of the first people Forman hired. Miller once said she was surprised how easily Forman was able to discover people's talents and put them to work: "Forman was, in my opinion, an organizational genius. He could find out in five minutes what you knew how to do, and in his mind he had a place for you to be. He was phenomenal."[35] When Miller told Forman that she could type, he had her take reports from field secretaries on what they were doing. And after Miller told Forman she was a writer, he assigned her to work with Julian Bond on the *Student Voice*, SNCC's newsletter.

Julian Bond described Forman's habit of refusing to take no for an answer when he wanted someone for SNCC. A senior at Morehouse, a black Atlanta college, Bond had been involved in SNCC sit-ins from the beginning. Bond recalled that after Forman found out Bond was a good writer, Forman demanded that Bond join SNCC as a staffer: "He invited/ordered me to write and produce [the *Student Voice*] and from then on I was hooked."[36] Forman was forceful enough to get Bond to quit school—finally getting his degree in 1971. Bond served as SNCC's communications director until 1965, when he was elected to the Georgia House of Representatives.

Brooks had told Forman that SNCC needed "a dictator to organize and pull strings and tell us what to do."[37] Once Forman hired people, he closely monitored SNCC workers throughout the South. He kept in constant contact with them, encouraged them, and advised them on how to handle the difficult situations they encountered. Bernard Lafayette Jr., a field secretary, said Forman would call field people and ask, "What's going on down there? I don't see anything in the newspaper. You all sleeping or what?"[38]

But Forman was not an elitist boss who just issued orders. He attended major protests, where he was arrested like everyone else. And visitors to SNCC's Atlanta headquarters often found him sweeping the floor or doing other janitorial work, such as painting the new, larger offices they moved into in May 1962. Some visitors to SNCC's office thought he was the janitor because he often wore bib overalls. Most SNCC workers wore jeans or overalls because that was how many of the poor, rural southern blacks they worked with dressed.

Forman also wrote articles about SNCC's work, kept in touch with other civil rights groups, and headed SNCC's fund-raising efforts. He built a national network of financial supporters by opening offices in major cities with large black populations, such

Julian Bond, left, and James Forman address the media at the Georgia state capitol. Forman persuaded the talented Bond to join SNCC as a staffer and writer.

Sweeping Floors

———————————————◼———————————————

Robert "Bob" Zellner, whose father and grandfather had both been members of the racist Ku Klux Klan (KKK), was the first white southerner to become a field secretary for the Student Nonviolent Coordinating Committee (SNCC). When Zellner first met James Forman, the SNCC executive secretary was sweeping the floors of SNCC's Atlanta office. Zellner recalls:

> On my first day at the office Forman met me at the door holding a broom in his outstretched hand. "Here, man, it's yo day on the broom." He met my perplexed look with a perfectly good explanation. In our new society . . . all the cats got to take they place on the broom. . . . "I just finished this front part but the back is waitin' for you." . . . Many a morning I arrived to see Jim sweeping the floor. He would silently pass me the broom as I meditated on what a few short months before would have been unthinkable, a fierce looking Black man handing me a broom! A born and raised young white southern male, daddy in the KKK, sweeping the floor in Atlanta because a Black man told me to.

Civil Rights Movement Veterans. "Tributes to and Memories of Jim Forman (1928–2005)." www.crm vet.org/mem/forman.htm.

as New York and Chicago. "Friends of SNCC" groups in those cities raised money to pay SNCC salaries and fund SNCC projects, including money to bail people out of jail when they were arrested.

Not long after Forman joined SNCC, he also helped to resolve a battle between SNCC staffers over the group's future.

Forman Solidifies SNCC

SNCC's focus since its creation in 1960 had been on direct-action events such as sit-ins and Freedom Rides. But despite the significant gains they had achieved in weakening segregation, some SNCC members began to believe that the best and fastest way to achieve equality was to enable blacks to vote. Even though the U.S. Constitution guaranteed all citizens that right, southern states had kept blacks from voting for decades, using laws and practices that made it almost impossible for them to even register to vote. Blacks who tried to register to vote had to pay poll taxes, pass difficult literacy tests, or meet other difficult requirements white officials waived for their fellow whites.

The split over SNCC's future revealed itself at the meeting Forman held his first weekend in Atlanta. In August, Ella Baker had suggested a compromise: to split SNCC into two wings, one to concentrate on direct action and the other to concentrate on voter registration. Forman eased the concerns of people from both wings by telling them that direct action like protests and marches would also be part of voter registration drives. Diane Nash was chosen to head direct-action efforts, and Charles Jones headed voter registration activity.

Forman's ability to heal the division between the two groups so they could continue to work together effectively was one of the strengths he brought to SNCC along with his organizational and management skills. Civil rights historian Joanne Grant says Forman was important in keeping SNCC united and in shaping the organization's future: "Forman arrived at SNCC at a crucial time. He was able to reconcile forces by applying his gruff assessment that whatever was happening in local areas (known as 'the field') was more important than whatever squabbles were taking place in the home office. He was able to maintain a sense of balance."[39]

"A Circle of Trust"

Forman's work with SNCC fulfilled his dream of working with a group of young people dedicated to fighting for black rights. In a 1962 SNCC meeting, Forman said he believed that the emotional ties that existed between SNCC members, who were all working toward a single goal were some of its greatest strengths. "[There was] an intense comradeship, born out of sacrifice and suffering and a commitment to the future, and out of knowledge that we were indeed challenging the political structure of the country, and out of a feeling that our basic strength rested in the energy, love, and warmth of the group. The band of sisters and brothers, in a circle of trust, felt complete at last."[40]

Chapter Four

SNCC and Voter Registration

The right to vote was the most powerful right southern whites denied African Americans because being able to vote would give them the political power they needed to be treated equally. The Fifteenth Amendment to the U.S. Constitution, which was ratified by states in 1870, guaranteed that no U.S. citizen could be denied the right to vote. Although blacks had been able to vote after the Civil War, in the last few decades of the nineteenth century, southern states had enacted laws that made it nearly impossible for African Americans to even register to vote.

White southerners used several methods to keep blacks from voting. Southern states approved poll taxes, a small tax whites could afford to pay but many poor blacks could not. Southern laws also established literacy tests that many blacks in the nineteenth and early twentieth centuries could not pass because of the lack of educational opportunities for blacks. Some literacy tests involved complicated questions about state constitutions. Although even most whites could not answer such questions, they were allowed to register anyway or did not need to take a test. Although the laws violated the Constitution, federal officials never stepped in to force southern states to allow blacks to vote. In addition, racist whites intimidated blacks from voting by beating or threatening death to any blacks who tried to register to vote. This disenfranchisement of black voters was clearly seen in Mississippi, where the restrictive laws had cut the number of eligible black voters from 190,000 in the late nineteenth century to just 2,000 in 1960, even though blacks made up 43 percent of the state's population.

In July 1961, New York educator Robert (Bob) Moses went to McComb, Mississippi, to begin the Student Nonviolent Coordinating Committee's first voter registration drive. SNCC historian Clayborne Carson claims his arrival "marked the beginning of SNCC's transition from its role as a coordinator of campus protest activities to one as the vanguard of a broad-based mass struggle in the deep South."[41] In the next few years, SNCC became the leader in the fight to give back the right to vote to black citizens.

SNCC conducts a training session for students participating in a voter registration drive. Robert Moses, second from left, and James Forman, right, coordinated the effort.

Like James Forman, Moses had been inspired by the civil rights struggle in the South to quit his high school job teaching mathematics in New York and come south to help southern blacks. But Moses soon discovered how hard it was to recruit local blacks to register to vote. He said McComb blacks were afraid to register because they had "a deeply entrenched habit of deference to, as well as genuine fear of, white power."[42] Moses himself quickly learned why they were so afraid of local whites.

White Violence

After weeks of talking to blacks in McComb and neighboring communities and attempting to help them register to vote, Moses had succeeded in registering only ten voters by August 13. On August 31, Moses was accompanying two more people to register to vote in Liberty, in Amite County, when several white men confronted him. Billy Jack Caston, a cousin of the county sheriff, viciously attacked Moses, hitting him with the handle of a knife. Moses needed nine stitches to close the bloody head wound. Moses then became the first black brave enough to file charges against a white man in Amite County since Reconstruction, a period that extended from the end of the Civil War in 1865 until 1877, during which the federal government used its military to protect the rights of black citizens in former Confederate states. An all-white jury, however, found Caston innocent despite the testimony of witnesses to the brutal attack on Moses.

The bravery Moses showed in challenging whites rallied McComb blacks to his cause. Burgland High School students as well as adults conducted the first protest marches and sit-ins ever held in McComb. Twelve-year-old Jessie Divens said she began participating in them because Moses had made her brave enough to challenge white rule. "I always knew I was equal to everybody else, and he came here to prove that to us. To me, it was a revolution that had started [and it was] something that I had to go be a part of or just burst wide open."[43]

White residents, led by the Ku Klux Klan, began attacking people involved in the civil rights campaign. They beat up people and fired gunshots at their homes at night. On September 25, 1961, a racist white fired a fatal shot to Herbert Lee, a black farmer involved in voter registration. The violence, and the inability of blacks to fight

Fannie Lou Hamer

On August 23, 1962, Fannie Lou Hamer attended a Student Nonviolent Coordinating Committee (SNCC) meeting in Ruleville, Mississippi, that changed her life. Hamer, who had never tried to vote, agreed to register to vote the next day. When she did, the owner of the plantation she lived on fired her and evicted her from her home. Hamer became one of SNCC's most valiant workers and a revered civil rights hero. She explains the decision she made:

> Until SNCC came I didn't know that a Negro could register and vote. [Bob Moses and James Forman] were some of the SNCC workers who ran that meeting. When they asked for those to raise their hands who'd go down to the courthouse the next day, I raised mine. Held it up as high as I could get it. I guess if I'd had any sense I'd a-been a little scared but what was the point of being scared? The only thing they could do to me was kill me and it seemed like they'd been trying to do that a little bit at a time ever since I could remember.

Quoted in Juan Williams. *Eyes on the Prize: America's Civil Rights Years, 1954–1965.* New York: Viking Penguin, 1987, pp. 177–178.

Fannie Lou Hamer joined SNCC in 1962 and became one of its most valiant workers and a revered civil rights hero.

An Albany, Georgia, policeman arrests two black men at the Trailways bus station in December 1962 for trying to get served at the lunch counter.

a racist legal system controlled by whites, doomed SNCC's initial attempt to register voters, and the project ended in December.

SNCC's venture into McComb, however, was only its first attempt at registering voters. The second began in Albany, Georgia, in October 1961, just a few weeks after the McComb drive had begun, and expanded into what became known as the Albany Movement.

A Community Rises Up

Albany was located in Dougherty County, which had a population of twenty-three thousand blacks and thirty-three thousand whites but only a few black voters. Forman sent SNCC field secretaries Charles Sherrod, Cordell Reagon, and Charles Jones to Albany to both register black voters and fight Jim Crow laws.

Forman said SNCC decided to do both in Albany because segregation there was so strict: "The technique varies from situation to situation. We don't really have a formalized approach. It was an experiment."[44]

SNCC recruited young people from Albany State College and Monroe High and Carver Junior High Schools to help in the campaign. On November 22, SNCC volunteers Bertha Gober and Blanton Hall were among five college students arrested in the Albany Trailways bus terminal when they tried to sit in the white waiting room. They were testing the federal rule integrating interstate travel facilities that had gone into effect on November 1. Gober said, "I felt [I] had a right to use all facilities [and that] it was necessary to show the people that human dignity must be obtained even if through suffering or maltreatment."[45] Her "suffering" included two nights in jail and suspension from college.

On December 10, Forman led four white and four black SNCC Freedom Riders from Atlanta to Albany on the Georgia Central Railroad. They integrated seating—that is, they sat together—on the trip without incident, but the black students were arrested in Albany for entering the white waiting room. They were charged with disturbing the peace but refused bail. Two days later, more than four hundred black high school and college students marched in protest of the arrests. Police chief Laurie Pritchett arrested all of them, saying, "We can't tolerate . . . SNCC or any other n****r organization to take over this town with mass demonstrations."[46]

More than seven hundred people were jailed in protests and marches as more and more Albany blacks began fighting for civil rights. Historian Lynne Olson writes that in Albany, "for the first time in the history of the civil rights movement, a direct action protest was supported by an entire black community, a large segment of which was in jail."[47] Media coverage of the mass arrests led Rev. Martin Luther King Jr. to come to Albany on December 15. King was arrested the next day during a protest march.

The national media attention King brought to Albany led city officials to agree to free jailed demonstrators. They also promised to desegregate travel facilities and to consider black complaints about segregation. After King was released from jail and had left town, Forman criticized him for accepting vague promises from city officials that they would treat blacks better in the future. When Albany officials failed to honor their promises, the protests were renewed, and hundreds more people were jailed. Protests against segregation continued through August 1962 but eventually ended. SNCC's Bill Hansen admitted years later that the protests had been a failure: "We were naïve enough to think we could fill up the jails. We ran out of people before [Pritchett] ran out of jails."[48]

Voter registration, however, was more successful. According to Slater King, an Albany Movement leader, SNCC succeeded in helping blacks register and awakened the political strength of the black community. He himself ran for mayor of Albany in 1963. Even though he lost that election, he said that the increasing numbers of black voters had made white officials more conciliatory to black demands. His candidacy, he wrote, "consolidated the Negro vote and formed one bloc unit where Negroes voted 90 per cent

When Martin Luther King Jr., second from left, was arrested in Albany, Georgia, by police chief Laurie Pritchett, right, it brought national attention and forced concessions by city officials.

together on all of the candidates."[49] SNCC registration projects in other areas of the South, however, often met with more resistance than in Albany.

Violence in Greenwood

In August 1962, SNCC joined with other civil rights groups to work with the federal Voter Education Project (VEP), which over the next six years provided more than $900,000 to fund voter registration campaigns. In 1963 SNCC began registering voters in Greenwood, Mississippi. On February 28, SNCC members Bob Moses and Jim Travis left the SNCC office with VEP's Randolph Blackwell. Whites in another car following them shot at them. Travis, who was hit in the head and shoulder but survived, explained what happened: "I felt something burn my ear. [They] had opened fire on us. It sounded like a machine gun. I felt something burn my ear and [I] yelled out that I had been shot. As I let

Freedom Schools

Student Nonviolent Coordinating Committee (SNCC) volunteers during the Mississippi Summer Project staffed forty-one Freedom Schools. About two thousand students attended the schools. In a July 11, 1964, letter to her parents, white SNCC teacher Pam Parker described her students' fierce desire to learn: "They want to learn so badly. We have no problem with attention drifting. Our problem is dismissing a group so it can go to another class. I feel so humble because the girls I work with are so wonderful. They are so eager to learn that I don't feel that I can ever begin to give them all that they are ready for."

One of the Freedom School students was Walter Saddler, who attended the Gluckstadt School until it burned down and then went to one in Canton. Saddler said the experience boosted his dream of attending college and made him believe he could succeed there. Saddler did eventually go to college. He became a reporter for WJTV in Jackson, Mississippi, and later became the station's vice president of news.

Pam Parker. "Three Letters from a Freedom School Teacher." Holly Springs, Mississippi, July 11, 1964. www.crmvet.org/info/chude-fs.htm.

go of the wheel, Moses grabbed hold of the wheel and brought the car to a stop on the shoulder of the highway."[50]

The next day Forman, Moses, and nine other SNCC workers were arrested in Greenwood while taking 150 blacks to register at the LeFlore County Courthouse. Police set dogs loose on the group and arrested the SNCC workers. From jail, Forman claimed that charges filed against them of "inciting to riot" and "refusing to move on" were false because they had only been trying to help blacks register. He declared that "the Student Nonviolent Coordinating Committee workers in LeFlore County are determined to stay until every eligible Negro is registered to vote!"[51]

Forman's promise was a bold one because Mississippi posed the greatest challenge to voting rights for blacks. When VEP began its campaign in 1962, only 1.4 million of the 5 million blacks of voting age in eleven southern states were registered to vote, but by 1964 that number had jumped to more than 2 million. However, in Mississippi only five thousand new voters had been registered because of intense white political resistance and racist violence. To overcome the South's most powerful brand of racism, SNCC banded together with other civil rights groups and local leaders in the Council of Federated Organizations (COFO) to stage a united, summer-long voter drive that became known as the Mississippi Summer Project.

Mississippi Summer Project

In the summer of 1964, more than one thousand volunteers flocked to Mississippi to help blacks register to vote. For Forman, the massive, powerful, and dramatic campaign was a dream come true. He noted: "The Mississippi Summer Project of 1964 [was] a culmination and high point of all the work SNCC had been doing since 1960. It represented a massing of forces and a consolidation of popular power perhaps unequalled in the history of American civil rights organizations."[52]

The vast majority of volunteers were college students from northern states, 90 percent of them white, who had been recruited and trained by SNCC. Moses, who directed the campaign, said the white volunteers were important to show southern whites it was not just African Americans who were willing to fight for the right of blacks to vote. Moses also said that a combined volunteer

As part of the SNCC-organized Mississippi Summer Project, federal voter registrars register black voters in Mississippi.

force of blacks and whites fit into SNCC's policy of brotherhood: "I always thought that the one thing [SNCC] can do for the country that no one else could do is to be above the race issue."[53]

From June 14 to June 27, volunteers attended orientation sessions at Western College for Women in Oxford, Ohio. In mock situations, SNCC workers subjected the trainees to the vocal and physical harassment they would face in marches and other situations. Forman even bluntly warned them: "I may be killed, you may be killed."[54] Volunteers who could not remain nonviolent in play-acting scenarios were sent home. Those who passed muster were spread out around Mississippi to educate blacks to pass literacy tests and perform other tasks to register. Volunteers had only the clothes and items they could carry. They were required to provide $150 for personal expenses and $500 for bail money.

Violence Greets SNCC Workers

The first volunteers left Oxford on June 20. The next day three civil rights workers who had been investigating the burning of a church near Philadelphia, Mississippi, disappeared—twenty-year-old Andrew Goodman and twenty-four-year-old Michael Schwerner, who were white, and twenty-four-year-old James Chaney of Meridian, Mississippi, who was black. Forty-four days later, their bodies were found. Members of the KKK had killed them by shooting and beating them to death with chains and mutilating their bodies. In 1967 seven men were convicted of their murders after the Federal Bureau of Investigation probed into the case. On June 21, 2005, Edgar Ray Killen was also found guilty of three counts of manslaughter in their deaths. He was found guilty on the forty-first anniversary of one of the most notorious incidents of violence during the 1960s civil rights era.

Their deaths were only the beginning of the worst outbreak of racist violence in Mississippi in nearly a century. Whites beat up eighty civil rights workers and murdered at least three other

The murder of SNCC workers Michael Schwerner, James Chaney, and Andrew Goodman by Ku Klux Klan members in June 1964 would become a turning point in the fight for civil rights.

SCHWERNER CHANEY GOODMAN

blacks even though they had not been part of the voter drive. There were thirty-five shooting incidents; sixty-five homes and buildings, including thirty-five churches, were bombed or set on fire. And more than one thousand people were arrested for protesting or trying to register to vote.

Some of the most intense violence was in McComb, where SNCC workers had returned after a three-year absence. On July 5, SNCC project director Curtis Hayes led six blacks and two whites to the home of Willie Mae Cotton, where they intended to open an office. Two nights later a bomb blew away part of the home; no one died, but Hayes was knocked unconscious, and white volunteer Dennis Sweeney suffered a concussion. On June 19, whites beat up Jehudah Menachem Mendel "Mendy" Samstein, a Jewish student from New York who was serving as a SNCC field secretary.

Forman Exposes Cruelty in Hattiesburg, Mississippi

The Student Nonviolent Coordinating Committee declared January 22, 1964, Freedom Day in Hattiesburg, Mississippi. James Forman accompanied blacks to the courthouse and managed to register twelve voters. Although it was raining, the sheriff made people stand outside the courthouse before registering. Knowing that reporters would write down his words, Forman pleaded through the closed door with the sheriff to let one elderly woman inside so she would not suffer in the downpour:

> Sheriff, will you be a Christian and let this old lady inside, a lady who has toiled in the fields of Forrest County many years, an old lady who now must stand out in the rain because she wants to register to vote? Is there no compassion in Forrest County for a woman seventy-one years old, whose feet are wet as she waits, who has nursed white children in her time, who can't even get a chair so she can sit down, for whom there is no room in the country courthouse?

Quoted in Howard Zinn. *SNCC: The New Abolitionists.* Boston: Beacon, 1964, p. 112.

Part of the Mississippi Summer Project included the formation of Freedom Schools to educate young people about how to fight for their rights. Most local blacks in McComb were too afraid to help at first, but a poem written at the McComb Freedom School by sixteen-year-old Joyce Brown shamed them into joining the effort. Brown wrote: "I asked for your churches, and you turned me down; But I'll do my work if I have to do it on the ground; You will not speak for fear of being heard, so you crawl in your shell and say, 'Do not disturb.'"[55] Brown's poem galvanized the community, which began offering churches and other buildings to civil rights workers, as well as raising $500, a large sum considering the poverty of McComb blacks. Despite continued violence, including nearly a dozen bombings, twenty-three people registered to vote on August 14. Registrar Glen Fortenberry arbitrarily denied all their applications.

A Failure

Despite the courage, dedication, and hard work of so many people, the Mississippi Summer Project succeeded in registering only twelve hundred voters. The problem was that the federal government still refused to step in and stop the white violence and the racist actions of law enforcement and other public officials who made it hard for blacks to register to vote. Federal officials would not take the decisive action needed to help blacks gain that precious right until one year later, when some of the most horrific violence in the history of the fight for civil rights occurred in Selma, Alabama.

Chapter Five

Selma, Alabama, and Sammy Younge Jr.

In November 1962, SNCC field secretary Bernard Lafayette Jr. asked James Forman for his own voter registration project. Forman said the only community open was Selma, Alabama, a town of about thirty thousand people. Although SNCC often sent people to communities in which racism was strong, Forman told Lafayette that SNCC had decided Selma was too dangerous. The reason was that Dallas County sheriff Jim Clark and his "posse," a volunteer group of racist whites, had been so fierce in using violence to keep blacks from gaining their rights that only 1 percent of Dallas County blacks were registered to vote.

The twenty-three-year-old SNCC veteran from Tampa, Florida, surprised Forman by enthusiastically responding, "That's great! I'd like to take that place."[56] Forman relented and allowed Lafayette and his wife, Colia, another SNCC worker, to go to Selma. The Lafayettes, who had only been married a few months, moved to Selma in February 1963 and began recruiting local blacks for the voter project. Local blacks, however, were wary of helping Lafayette because they feared white violence. On June 12, Lafayette had just returned home from a voter registration meeting when two white men attacked him. They struck him on the head repeatedly with a gun, opening a deep wound that bled freely and required six stitches. A neighbor who heard Lafayette's screams saved his life when he ran out of his home with a shotgun and scared away the assailants.

Lafayette's beating came on the same night civil rights leader Medgar Evers was shot to death in Jackson, Mississippi. Both

The funeral procession of murdered civil rights worker Medgar Evers winds through the streets of Jackson, Mississippi, on June 15, 1963. SNCC member Bernard Lafayette was beaten by the Klan in Selma, Alabama, the same day.

brutal acts occurred just hours after President John F. Kennedy had delivered a major speech on television backing civil rights; the violent attacks were considered warnings from racist whites that they would not let Kennedy help blacks win those rights. The next day black lawyer James Chestnut saw Lafayette in Selma with a bloody shirt and bruised and swollen face. Chestnut told him to go home and get cleaned up but Lafayette said, "No way. This is the symbol we need."[57] Lafayette viewed his wounds and bloody clothing as a badge of honor that signified he would never back down from racist whites. Lafayette's bravery made him a hero and emboldened local blacks to join SNCC's initial foray into one of the South's most racist areas.

Focusing on Selma

SNCC's Selma voter drive was summed up by the slogan "One Man, One Vote." In pursuit of that goal, SNCC on October 7, 1963, organized a Freedom Day in which workers led more than three hundred blacks to the Selma courthouse to register to vote. Blacks had to wait in line in the hot sun for hours to register instead of being allowed inside like whites. While they waited, Clark and his deputies photographed them to intimidate them.

As the day dragged on, Forman pleaded with Clark to allow SNCC to give people in line water and sandwiches. Despite Clark's refusal, Forman ordered Avery Williams and Chico Neblett to hand out food and water that SNCC had purchased. When they tried to do that, the SNCC workers were knocked to the ground, beaten with clubs, shocked with cattle prods, and arrested. At a rally that night, Forman said the day had been successful despite the fact that only a few blacks had been able to register to vote: "We ought to be happy today because we did something great. Jim Clark never saw that many [blacks] down there! Yeah, there was Jim Clark, rubbin' his head and his big fat belly; he was shuffling today like *we* used to!"[58]

White resistance was so strong and brutal that by the fall of 1964 only 335 of 15,115 blacks of voting age in Dallas County had been registered. In late 1964, James Bevel and Diane Nash, two of SNCC's founding members who now worked for the Southern Christian Leadership Conference, persuaded the SCLC to join SNCC's ongoing effort in Selma. The two groups began a

Martin Luther King Jr. speaks at the funeral of Jimmie Lee Jackson in Marion, Alabama. It was at this funeral that the idea for a march from Selma to Montgomery was conceived.

series of protests and other events that began on January 2, 1965, with a speech by Rev. Martin Luther King Jr. The most famous figure in civil rights history told nine hundred people at Brown Chapel African Methodist Episcopal Church to be prepared to march and possibly be arrested. The purpose for their actions, King declared, was to demand their vote and to force the federal government to protect their constitutional right to vote.

In the next two months, hundreds of blacks were arrested in a series of marches, protests, and sit-ins. King himself was jailed on February 1 after he led 250 people to the courthouse to register to vote. Clark and his deputies were brutal toward blacks brave enough to register. One of them was fifty-four-year-old Amelia Boynton, a local civil rights leader. On January 19 after Boynton refused Clark's humiliating order to go to the rear of the courthouse to wait to register, Clark grabbed the small black woman and repeatedly pushed her down the street while arresting her. But a few days later, Clark met his match in Annie Lee Cooper. When Clark tried to intimidate the Selma woman while she was waiting in line, Cooper boldly declared: "Ain't nobody scared around here."[59] When Clark shoved her, the large, strong 235-pound woman (107kg) punched him in the head. Three deputies then forced Cooper to the ground and Clark hit her with his billy club. Pictures of the cruel treatment of Boynton and Cooper appeared in newspapers across the nation.

Clark showed his brutal nature again on February 10 when he arrested more than 160 teenagers marching to the courthouse. Before taking them to jail, Clark and his deputies used clubs and cattle prods to herd them on a forced run of more than two miles (3.2km). "March, dammit, march!," Clark shouted. "You want to march so bad, now you can march. Let's go!"[60] When a fifteen-

Sheriff Jim Clark arrests Annie Lee Cooper in a voter registration line after she punched him for shoving her after she resisted his attempt to intimidate her.

SNCC and SCLC

———————◾———————

The Southern Christian Leadership Conference (SCLC) played a big part in the birth of the Student Nonviolent Coordinating Committee (SNCC). James Forman, however, did not always like working with the SCLC, as SNCC had to do in Selma, Alabama. Forman's main concern was that Rev. Martin Luther King Jr.'s celebrity overshadowed the work the SCLC did. Forman did not believe it was right to have one person become the symbol of such a civil rights group because the loss of that person could weaken or destroy it. He later explained:

> We felt that there should be a projection and an organization of in-digenous leadership and leadership from the community. Whereas the Southern Christian Leadership Conference took the position that Martin was a charismatic leader who was mainly responsible for raising money and they raised [the] most money off of his lead-ership. But these differences in leadership then led to differences in style of work. We wanted a movement that would survive the loss of our lives; therefore, the necessity to build a broad based move-ment and not just a charismatic leader.

Quoted in Public Broadcasting Service. *Eyes on the Prize: America's Civil Rights Movement, 1954–1985.* "Bridge to Freedom (1965)." www.pbs.org/wgbh/amex/eyesontheprize/about/pt_106.html.

year-old boy complained, a deputy hit him in the mouth with a billy club. By the time Clark let the youths slow down, many were so exhausted and sick they began vomiting.

The voting registration drive—and the violence—spilled over into neighboring communities. In nearby Marion, on February 18, SCLC leader Rev. C.T. Vivian spoke at a meeting at Zion Chapel United Methodist Church about having been punched in the mouth by Clark at the Selma courthouse two days earlier. When the meeting ended, Alabama state troopers and local police beat up blacks as they were leaving the church. One of the state troopers shot and killed twenty-six-year-old Jimmie Lee Jackson, who was trying to protect an elderly woman knocked down by the police.

At Jackson's funeral on February 28, Bevel proposed a march from Selma to Montgomery, the state capital, to protest Jackson's death and dramatize the battle for voting rights. His request set the stage for one of the most violent and dramatic episodes in civil rights history.

The Selma March

The 54-mile (87km) protest walk was scheduled for Sunday March 7. Forman opposed the march "because of the likelihood of police brutality."[61] SNCC voted against participating in the march but allowed individual members to join it. When King announced he would not be able to be at the march, however, Forman changed his plans. He realized King's absence would embolden racist whites to attack marchers because there would not be as much news coverage without King. So Forman ordered SNCC workers to be ready to rescue marchers injured by violence. Unfortunately, Forman's worst fears were realized in a day of ugly violence that gave rise to the nickname "Bloody Sunday."

At 12:30 P.M. on March 7, SNCC chairman John Lewis and the SCLC's Hosea Williams led about six hundred people from Brown Chapel to the Edmund Pettus Bridge, over which U.S. Route 80 led east out of Selma to Montgomery. After crossing the bridge, which spanned the Alabama River, marchers were confronted on the other side by a wall of state troopers, deputies, and Clark's "posse" members lined up shoulder-to-shoulder across four lanes of the highway. Marchers were ordered to turn back. When they did not do so immediately, law enforcement officers and civilians attacked them. The attackers began by firing tear gas into the crowd of men, women, and children, blinding and choking them. Then troopers on horseback charged into the marchers, swinging their clubs. Policemen and posse members carrying clubs, whips, and chains also attacked the marchers.

A mounted trooper struck Lewis on the head; he tried to protect himself but was knocked unconscious by a second blow. Eight-year-old Sheyann Webb saw men on horses charging through the cloud of stinging tear gas: "They had those awful masks on [and] I just turned and ran."[62] As Webb began running, she suddenly felt someone pick her up and carry her—it was Williams, who took her to safety. Boynton later recalled the horrendous scene: "The horses were more humane than the troopers; they stepped over fallen victims. As I stepped aside from a trooper's club, I felt a blow on my arm. Another blow by a trooper, as I was gasping for breath, knocked me to the ground and there I lay, unconscious."[63]

On March 21, 1965, 3,200 people walk across the Edmund Pettus Bridge in Selma, Alabama, to begin the historic march to Montgomery.

Bloody Sunday

◼

Student Nonviolent Coordinating Committee chairman John Lewis was knocked unconscious while leading marchers out of Selma, Alabama, on March 7, 1965, the day that became known as "Bloody Sunday." Lewis describes the vicious attack that day by Alabama state troopers, Dallas County sheriff's deputies, and civilians:

> It was a very peaceful, orderly protest. [But then the] troopers and members of Sheriff Clark's posse on horseback [came] toward us with billy clubs, tear gas, and bullwhips, trampling us with horses. I felt like it was the last demonstration, the last protest on my part, like I was going to take my last breath from the tear gas. I saw people rolling, heard people screaming and hollering. We couldn't go forward. If we tried to go forward we would've gone into the heat of battle. We couldn't go to the side, to the left, or to the right because we would have been going into the Alabama river, so we were beaten back down the streets of Selma, back to the church.

Quoted in Henry Hampton and Steve Fayer. *Voices of Freedom: An Oral History of the Civil Rights Movement from the 1950s Through the 1980s.* New York: Bantam Books, 1990, pp. 227–228.

John Lewis goes down under police billy clubs at the Edmund Pettus Bridge in Selma, Alabama, on Bloody Sunday, March 7, 1965.

Lewis and Boynton were among seventeen marchers hospitalized with injuries. News media accounts of the racist attack on peaceful marchers shocked the nation, but the violence failed to deter Selma blacks. Two weeks later, on March 21, about thirty-two hundred people, blacks and whites, resumed the march. The huge crowd crossed the bridge without resistance and for the next four days a smaller group of about three hundred continued walking toward Montgomery. The marchers made it to Montgomery on March 25 and held a victory rally at the capitol.

When the peaceful rally ended, volunteers began giving people rides back to Selma. Viola Liuzzo, a white mother of five from Detroit, was a volunteer driver. After dropping some people off in Selma, she and black teenager Leroy Moton, another volunteer, headed back to Montgomery to pick up more people who were returning to Selma. In Lowndes County, a car with four Ku Klux Klan members pulled up alongside Liuzzo's car and fired shots—Liuzzo was hit and her car careened off the highway. Moton survived but Liuzzo died in an ugly ending to a victorious day for blacks.

Victory and More Violence

The violence of "Bloody Sunday" along with the murders of Jackson and Liuzzo finally made the federal government act to ensure that African Americans in the South could exercise a right the U.S. Constitution guaranteed every American. On March 15, President Lyndon B. Johnson proposed the Voting Rights Act of 1965, which put in place safeguards that prevented whites from stopping blacks from registering to vote. Congress, which in the past had rejected similar legislation, approved the bill on August 6. Within a year, nine thousand Dallas County blacks had registered and were able to vote Clark out of office. By 1970, there were an estimated 3.5 million new black voters in the South, and their political power helped them end Jim Crow and elect officials, both black and white, who would treat them justly.

SNCC continued to battle for black rights because winning the right to vote did not immediately end racist treatment in the South. Liuzzo's death had occurred in Lowndes County, which was known as "Bloody Lowndes" because of its history of racist violence. Her death spurred SNCC to begin the Lowndes County

Freedom Project, which helped blacks register to vote, and in 1966 black candidates began running for local office in the county. In 1970 SNCC's work helped John Hullet to be elected as the county's first black sheriff.

SNCC's work was not easy because whites continued to use violence to stop black voting. On January 4, 1966, SNCC worker Sammy Younge Jr., a twenty-two-year-old navy veteran and student at the Tuskegee Institute in Tuskegee, Alabama, was murdered. Earlier in the day, a Macon County official had threatened Younge with a knife for trying to register voters. That night, Younge was shot to death when he tried to use a white bathroom in a gas station. Younge was the first black college student to die while fighting for black rights, and his death ignited protest marches by thousands of people. SNCC issued a stinging criticism of the federal government for failing to protect people fighting for their civil rights. In a statement issued by SNCC's Atlanta office, Chairman Lewis declared, "If the federal government cannot provide protection for people seeking civil rights [then] people will have no protection but themselves. We find it increasingly difficult to ask the people of the Black Belt to remain nonviolent. We have asked the President for federal marshals for over three years. If our plea is not answered, we have no choice."[64]

The group's reconsideration of nonviolence as a tactic was not an empty threat. Many blacks were beginning to abandon the principle of nonviolence because they believed they had a right to defend themselves. One of them was Forman.

Forman and Nonviolence

Forman was in New York when he learned of Younge's death. He was so deeply affected that in 1968 he wrote a book about it. In *Sammy Younge Jr.: The First Black College Student to Die in the Black Liberation Movement*, Forman said his belief in nonviolence to achieve civil rights had been weakened by years of being subjected to violence by white racists. He wrote: "In many ways the murder of Sammy Younge marked the end of tactical nonviolence: the long marches where blacks were expected to undergo harsh treatment by white Southern crackers, not protecting themselves, not fighting back—that day was over. When it occurs today, nonviolence is but the lingering edge of a phase in the struggle [for black rights]."[65]

James Forman Gets Angry

———————————◼———————————

On March 16, 1965, James Forman led a group of college students in Montgomery, Alabama, to protest violence against African Americans in Selma who were fighting for the right to vote. Eight students were hospitalized when law enforcement officials, some mounted on horses, used whips, canes, and cattle prods to brutally break up the demonstration at the state capitol. That night in Selma, an angry Forman condemned President Lyndon B. Johnson for failing to stop the continuing violence against blacks. In a speech in which he used profanity, Forman declared:

> There's only one man in the country that can stop [Alabama governor] George Wallace and those posses. These problems will not be solved until the man in that shaggedy old place called the White House [gets] on the phone and says, "Now listen, George, we're coming down there and throw you in jail if you don't stop that mess." . . . I said it today, and I will say it again, "If we can't sit at the table of democracy, we'll knock the f--king legs off!"

Quoted in John Lewis with Michael D'Orso. *Walking with the Wind: A Memoir of the Movement.* New York: Simon & Schuster, 1998, p. 341.

Although Forman had always adhered to SNCC's concept of nonviolence, he had also believed that blacks had a right to meet violence with violence to defend themselves against racist whites. In his autobiography, Forman discusses how he viewed nonviolence: "I saw violence or nonviolence as just different forms of struggle. At various points in a people's struggle they will use one form and then another. So long as one did not advocate nonviolence dogmatically, to be used at all times and all places, I could work with it."[66]

A growing lack of faith in nonviolence was only one of the philosophical changes taking place in the ranks of SNCC. A second, an embracing of the philosophy of Black Power, would ultimately destroy the group that had done so much to help blacks achieve equality.

Chapter Six

Life as a Snick

James Forman and Robert Moses were African American elementary-school teachers from Chicago and New York, respectively. Diane Nash and Charles McDew were blacks from northern states who attended black colleges in the South. Alabama native Robert Zellner came from a white family with a racist heritage. Danny Lyon was a white history major at the University of Chicago. Hollis Watkins and sixteen-year-old Cordell Reagon, who Forman called "the baby of the movement,"[67] were southern blacks. They were all Snicks—a name derived from the pronunciation of the initials of the Student Nonviolent Coordinating Committee (SNCC). Despite differences in race and social background, they and hundreds of other Snicks joined together to commit themselves to defeating the powerful, often sadistic racism that had denied southern blacks equality with whites since the end of the Civil War a century earlier.

To accomplish this goal, the group Forman lovingly described as a "band of sisters and brothers, in a circle of trust"[68] endured poverty-level living conditions, the constant threat of violence or harassment by racist whites, and even the disapproval of their own families. They were jailed, beaten, and killed. Through it all, they refused to quit despite the dangers and hardships they encountered. Their motivations were as varied as the Snicks were different from one another.

Joining SNCC

It was easy for James Forman to decide to quit his teaching job in Chicago to head south—he had experienced Jim Crow racism as a child and was already involved in civil rights work. It was harder for Robert Moses, who had grown up in New York, was teaching at the prestigious Horace Mann School, and only knew about the southern fight against racism through news media accounts. Yet Moses also decided to go south and risk his life over and over again in Mississippi. Moses said he did it because the bravery of the southern blacks awakened in him his own personal

Hollis Watkins, shown here in 2007, became a SNCC member after the Woolworth's boycott in 1961. Watkins says his bold stand against racism alienated some of his relatives, who feared white reprisals for his activism.

desire to fight racism: "Before, the Negro in the South had always looked on the defensive, cringing. This time they were taking the initiative. They were kids my age, and I knew this had something to do with my own life. It made me realize that for a long time I had been troubled by the problem of being a Negro and at the same time being an American."[69]

Diane Nash was one of many northern blacks who attended a black college in the South. The Chicago native was a student at Fisk University in Nashville, Tennessee, when she first experienced Jim Crow segregation at the 1959 Tennessee State Fair. Nash became angry when she was forced to use the bathroom designated COLORED WOMEN, which was dirty and run-down compared with the white facility. The racist treatment led her to become a sit-in leader the following year. Charles McDew, a high school football player in Massillon, Ohio, was a freshman at South Carolina State College in Orangeburg when he had a brutal introduction to southern racism. A policeman who had stopped McDew while he was driving broke his jaw with a nightstick because McDew had failed to address him as "sir." McDew was also upset when white Christian churches refused to let him attend their services. As a result, McDew turned to the Jewish faith, which readily accepted him. His study of Judaism led him to this saying by Rabbi Hillel: "If I am not for myself, who will be for me? If I am only for myself, what am I? And if not now, when?"[70] That quotation inspired the future SNCC chairman to join the sit-ins.

Although Robert Zellner's father and grandfather had both been members of the white supremacist Ku Klux Klan (KKK), Zellner became one of the few southern whites who actively opposed racist treatment of blacks. Zellner, SNCC's first white field secretary, explained that growing up in the South, "you either capitulated absolutely and completely [to Jim Crow] or you became a rebel, a complete outlaw, and that's the way I went."[71] Zellner's father changed his racist views in later life, but his KKK grandfather once threatened to shoot his grandson if he ever saw him fighting for black rights.

Danny Lyon was an amateur photographer who wanted to use his camera to chronicle the fight for civil rights. When Lyon went to Albany, Georgia, in August 1962 to volunteer his services,

Forman immediately put him to work. Forman told Lyon to go to the courthouse and shoot pictures of the big water cooler for whites and the small one for African Americans, an assignment that would have been dangerous for a black photographer. Lyon became SNCC's official photographer in 1963. He said that Forman was responsible for his pictures, which appeared in publications around the world: "James Forman would direct me, protect me, and at times fight for a place for me in the movement. He is directly responsible for my pictures existing at all."[72]

Cordell Reagon was a sixteen-year-old student at Pearl High School in Nashville, Tennessee, when the sit-ins began in February 1960. Although college students felt high school students were too young to protest, Reagon and other students walked out of Pearl High one day and joined in a protest march that was passing their school: "[We] wanted to do something, 'cause we thought it would be fun if for no other reason. We didn't have

Robert Zellner Is Beaten

———— ■ ————

Robert Zellner's introduction to life as a Student Nonviolent Coordinating Committee worker was a severe beating by a white mob in McComb, Mississippi. On October 4, 1961, Zellner participated in a protest march in which 116 high school students were arrested. Zellner said racist whites were angered to see a white person marching with black students:

> People just couldn't believe it when they saw me. They went into a level of hysteria. . . . [There] was a vanguard of the mob, about ten or a dozen white men, and they began to gather round me and hit me. They would take a swing at me and they would not look for my reaction but they would look for the reaction of the cops. And the cops very clearly with their body language and everything else said, "Sure, get that son of a bitch." [When Charles McDew and Bob Moses tried to protect Zellner] the first action of the police was to come over and get them and beat them with blackjacks.

Quoted in Henry Hampton and Steve Fayer. *Voices of Freedom: An Oral History of the Civil Rights Movement from the 1950s Through the 1980s*. New York: Bantam Books, 1990, p. 145.

any politics, but we wanted to do something [to fight racism]."[73] Reagon later became a SNCC field secretary.

Hollis Watkins was born in Lincoln County, Mississippi. In 1961, at the age of twenty, Watkins joined a sit-in at a Woolworth's in McComb, Mississippi, and later helped Moses register voters there. Watkins said his bold stand against racism angered not only whites but some of his relatives, who feared that his activism might endanger them. "[They] would see me walking down the street and then they would pass over to the other side rather than meet me on the street. Because they were afraid of what white people might do to them because they were my relatives."[74]

It was hard for some people to join SNCC because they had to give up important things such as jobs and family relationships. They soon discovered that life was even harder as a Snick.

Daily Life in SNCC

As part of SNCC's fundamental strategy, SNCC workers tried to become part of the communities they were sent to so they could persuade local citizens to help them fight racism. When Moses went to McComb in July 1960 to begin registering voters, he set the pattern for future field secretaries on how to do that. He recalls: "For two weeks I did nothing but [talk] to the business leaders, the ministers, the people [asking] them if they would support ten students who would come to work on a voter registration drive. [When students arrived] we went around house-to-house, door-to-door, in the hot sun every day because the most important thing was to convince the local townspeople that we were people who were responsible."[75]

To cement their relationship with local residents, SNCC workers and volunteers often lived in private homes. That meant they shared the living conditions of poor southern blacks, which included using primitive outdoor toilets. Don Jelinek, a lawyer who worked for SNCC for three years, and Jean Wiley, a black student at Morgan State College, reminisced about that experience during a 2008 discussion with other former Snicks: "Don [Jelinek]: I mean, I remember my first night in a sharecropper's shack. I asked where the toilet was. [Laughter] Jean [Wiley]: So did I. [Laughter] Don: And then, I started looking for the switch on the

A group of SNCC members at a Mississippi sit-in. SNCC members often stayed in private homes and shared meager living conditions with poor southern blacks, which cemented their relationship with local residents.

wall for the lights. [Laughter] Now I knew all about poverty intellectually, but it had never gotten through to me."[76]

During the summer of 1962, a small group of women was working on a voter registration project in Lee County, Georgia. They had so little money, they were forced to work odd jobs to buy food. Penny Patch, a white student from Swarthmore College, wrote about their plight in SNCC's *Student Voice*: "We do not have the money to pay for gas or wear and tear. We can see no other way out than to attempt to raise money by washing cars, dishes, floors, and windows, cutting grass, or any other chores. . . . We are not supermen. We are only young people with a determination to be FREE and to be FREE NOW!"[77]

The Snicks won the trust of southern blacks by sharing their difficult lifestyles, such as using smelly wooden outhouses. During the 1964 Mississippi Summer Project, one older black woman

Freedom Singers

Singing protest songs such as "We Shall Overcome" was a part of nearly every civil rights rally and protest. The Student Nonviolent Coordinating Committee (SNCC) seized on singing as both a tactic to make people more enthusiastic about the cause of racial justice and to raise money. Cordell Reagon and his wife, Bernice Johnson Reagon, were among the founders in 1962 of the Freedom Singers, who sang at major civil rights events and toured the nation to give concerts. Bernice explains how she changed the wording of traditional black songs such as "Over My Head, I See Trouble in the Air" to reflect the fight for civil rights:

> I put in *freedom* [for trouble], and by the second line everyone was singing, with me placing a new word (*glory*, *justice*, and so forth) for each cycle. . . . I could change the text to articulate and support what we were trying to do in fighting segregation. . . . In the Movement there was a transformation that took place inside of the people, and the singing echoed it.

Quoted in Faith S. Holsaert et al., eds. *Hands on the Freedom Plow: Personal Accounts by Women in SNCC.* Urbana: University of Illinois Press, 2010. p. 147.

The Freedom Singers, from left to right, Charles Neblett, Bernice Reagon, Cordell Reagon, and Rutha Harris sang at SNCC events and toured the nation giving concerts.

explained how much she appreciated white SNCC volunteers who endured hardships to help African Americans: "These young white folks who are already free, they come here only to help us. They is proving to us that black and white can do it together, that it ain't true what we always thought, that all white folks is [bad] 'cause they sure is not."[78]

In addition to being unpleasant at times, life as a Snick could also be dangerous because the members of SNCC daily faced the threat of violence.

Dangerous Times

The men and women who engaged in sit-ins, protests, marches, and voter registration work all knew that they might be brutalized by racist whites. Even Nash, one of the leaders of the Nashville sit-ins, admitted that she was afraid about what would happen when she began trying to desegregate lunch counters in Nashville: "This is Tennessee, and white people down here are *mean*. We are going to come up against white Southern men who are forty and fifty and sixty years old, who are politicians and judges and owners of businesses, and I am twenty-two-years old. What am I *doing*? And how is this little group of students my age going to stand up to these powerful people?"[79]

Their determination to defeat racism helped Nash and other Snicks to conquer their fears. But fear of white violence, which was only sporadic, was only a part of the anxiety. John Lewis, who became SNCC's chairman in 1963 when McDew stepped down, wrote that SNCC workers were more often bored and tired during long marches and protests than fearful of white retaliation. Lewis noted that it took a great deal of fortitude to face long hours of discomfort and exhaustion: "The patience and persistence it took to endure those countless hours of sheer boredom in stifling heat or bone-chilling cold, in driving rain and wet, slushy snow, was as admirable as the bravery it took to face the billy clubs of those deputies."[80]

During the civil rights era, danger materialized all too often. Southern whites cursed and spit at Snicks, beat them, jailed them, and burned and shot at them in their homes or their offices. In September 1962 in Lee County, Georgia, three people were injured when whites shot into a home housing SNCC voter registration workers. Jack Chatfield, a white student from Connecticut, was shot twice in the arm. Christopher Allen, a white student from Oxford, England, and Prathia Hall, an African American from Philadelphia, were both grazed by bullets.

During a march to city hall in Albany, Georgia, in June 1963, white firemen and police unwound high-pressure hoses to sweep demonstrators off the building's front steps. It was one of the most terrifying experiences that Dorothy Miller, a white volunteer from New York, said she had had in the years she worked for SNCC. She said Forman came to their rescue that day: "He saved our lives. We were getting ready to be killed. Just at that moment, Forman jumped up from among the demonstrators and walked straight at the police [and shouted,] 'Now wait a minute. What's going on here?'"[81] Forman distracted the whites long enough for demonstrators to leave and avoid being pummeled by high-pressure jets of water.

Miller was one of many women who played an important role in SNCC's history. Nevertheless, the women's male counterparts often failed to treat them as equals even though they were all fighting for equality.

Women in SNCC

Ella Baker was the catalyst for SNCC's creation in 1960. Jane Stembridge was SNCC's first paid worker. Nash was one of SNCC's founding members and the person most responsible in 1961 for continuing the Freedom Rides after violence in Alabama nearly stopped them. Despite the many impressive contributions that women made to SNCC's success, some male Snicks treated them as inferiors, mainly because they were infected with the sexist views prevalent then in U.S. culture. Even Nash, a heroic civil rights figure, admitted she sometimes had trouble dealing with men: "I was the only female in this group of good old boys [and] sexism was a serious issue. They regarded me as this troublesome female who [was] a pain in the neck and causing really unnecessary problems."[82]

The issue of sexist treatment of women came to a head in two incidents in 1964. The first was a sit-in that spring by five female staff workers who were protesting conditions in Forman's Atlanta office. The protesters included Forman's wife, Mildred.

Ella Baker was the catalyst for SNCC's creation in 1960. She would later join and lead the Southern Conference Education Fund, where she is shown here.

The women sang the civil rights song "We Shall Not Be Moved" and held signs saying "Unfair" and "Now." One of the participants, Mary King, said that Forman "looked baffled and none too pleased when he saw us, but we talked it out."[83] Forman, who was generally considered to be sensitive to the role of women in SNCC, agreed to several changes. One was that women would not always be assigned to take notes at meetings.

At a staff retreat in November 1964 in Waveland, Mississippi, King and other SNCC women presented a paper that described the unfair treatment that they resented. The statement claimed that women were passed over for leadership positions and were expected to do traditional female roles like making coffee and getting food. The most serious charge was that the men did not respect their opinions. Fay Bellamy claimed that "even though the women were in the meetings the men seemed to have the final opinion."[84] Judy Richardson, a black woman from Tarrytown, New York, said, however, that "whatever sexism I found in SNCC was always, for me, balanced by an unbelievable sense of power. And that was nurtured in me as much by the men as by the women of SNCC."[85]

Male Snicks grumbled about and ridiculed the complaints, and not much changed; however, the female SNCC uprising is cited as one of the sparks that ignited the modern women's rights movement in the 1960s.

Stress Fells James Forman

James Forman was under more pressure than anyone in the Student Nonviolent Coordinating Committee (SNCC). In addition to the constant worry about being jailed or attacked that he shared with everyone else, Forman had to oversee SNCC's operations. His worries included financial concerns. On June 1, 1963, SNCC had a $10,000 deficit, but over the course of the rest of that year, Forman raised almost $50,000, which he used to establish new projects in several states. Stress finally caught up with Forman in January 1963 when he was hospitalized for a bleeding ulcer and nearly died. Forman once explained that stress affected everyone in SNCC:

> Stress of the kind that our workers experienced in the . . . South surely takes its toll—sooner or later. . . . I have seen many— including myself—work under intense stress without taking the time to renew their energy with rest periods or removal from the scene of action. The day-to-day demands have been so great that people felt they could not take time out. Burning with anxiety, confused from exhaustion, these revolutionaries still refused to rest.

James Forman. *The Making of Black Revolutionaries*. Seattle: University of Washington Press, 2000, pp. 291–292.

They Felt Like Soldiers

At the age of fifteen, Cleveland Sellers organized the first sit-in protest in his hometown of Denmark, South Carolina. Sellers later worked for SNCC. After the 1964 Mississippi Summer Project, many people asked Sellers what it had been like trying to register voters in a state hostile to black rights. Sellers said that he realized then how dramatic the experience had been for him: "For the first time in my life, I understood how soldiers feel when they return from wars and have to grope unwillingly for answers to the terribly innocent 'How was it?'"[86] Sellers realized that he had been fighting a war and that the enemy had been racism. His fellow Snicks were also soldiers in that conflict.

Chapter Seven

SNCC and Black Power

Jim Crow meant that African Americans were barred from most southern colleges, including state-run schools that should have been open to any resident. On October 1, 1962, two people died in violent protests that erupted when James Meredith became the first African American admitted to the University of Mississippi. Meredith endured racist treatment—he had to be guarded by federal marshals in order to attend classes—and graduated to become a civil rights hero. Almost four years later on June 5, 1966, Meredith began a solitary, 220-mile (354-km) March Against Fear from Jackson, Mississippi, to Memphis, Tennessee. The next day, a racist white firing a shotgun wounded but failed to kill Meredith. In response to the attempted murder of the civil rights hero, the Student Nonviolent Coordinating Committee and other groups continued the walk.

Before the march began, SNCC field secretary Willie Ricks asked James Forman if he could use the phrase *Black Power* in speeches during the march to energize people. In his autobiography, Forman wrote that he gave Ricks his approval. "'Black Power—sure, try it,' I told him. 'Why not? After all, you'd only be shortening the phrase we are always using—power for poor black people. "Black Power" is shorter and means the same thing. Go on, try it.' And that is how the cry for black power came to be voiced."[87]

Several hundred blacks and whites continued the march from where Meredith had been shot, sleeping in tents or on the ground at night and being fed by supporters in communities they passed through. Ricks used the phrase several times during the march, but it was Stokely Carmichael who made it famous on the evening of June 16 in Greenwood, Mississippi. Carmichael had been arrested earlier in the day for trespassing on public property when marchers tried to camp at Stone Street Negro Elementary School. After Carmichael was released, he returned and gave an angry speech to marchers: "This is the twenty-seventh time I have been arrested and I ain't going to jail no more! The only way we gonna stop them white men from whuppin' us is to take over. What we gonna start sayin' now is Black Power!"[88]

The phrase was not new—Richard Wright titled his 1954 book about emerging African nations *Black Power,* and other blacks had

James Meredith grimaces in pain after being shot in Mississippi while leading his March Against Fear. After having the wound treated, Evers finished the march.

used it occasionally since. But Carmichael made it popular. The news media reported on his use of the phrase during his fiery speech and noted that other blacks had joyously shouted it back at him when he asked if that was what they wanted.

The simple phrase would ignite a new phase in the struggle for black rights throughout the nation; however, it had already begun to radically alter SNCC.

Black Power and SNCC

Carmichael had not bothered to consult Forman about using the term because Carmichael had become SNCC's chairman, and Forman was no longer its executive secretary. During a weekend meeting May 14–15, 1966, in Kingston, Tennessee, SNCC members had elected Carmichael to replace John Lewis as chairman and Ruby Doris Smith to succeed Forman as executive secretary.

Forman had decided to step down, but the ouster of Lewis was shocking because he was a well-known civil rights figure. Carmichael was respected for what he had done for SNCC for five years, especially his work in Lowndes County in 1965 when he led the drive that registered 2,669 black voters in a county that had none before then. But the main reason Lewis was being replaced was a change that was taking place among many blacks in SNCC and throughout the nation. The dramatic psychological shift in the way blacks viewed their struggle for equality was symbolized by the phrase *Black Power*.

In the past, blacks' lack of political and economic power had forced them to rely on whites, who controlled the government, to grant them equality. As the civil rights movement of the 1960s progressed, many blacks came to believe they had enough power themselves to seize those rights through the ballot box and their own social and economic strength. It was a dynamic psychological shift; they believed they should be able to decide their own future. Snicks who had adopted that Black Power philosophy voted Lewis out because they believed he still clung to the older, less militant belief about how blacks should secure their rights. And Forman was one of them. He asserted, "Those two words electrified the nation and the world. [We] had moved to the level of verbalizing our drive for power—not

Black Power and Whites

━━━━━━━━━━━━━━━ ■ ━━━━━━━━━━━━━━━

The Student Nonviolent Coordinating Committee (SNCC) issued a statement in 1966 that explained why it believed in the new, more militant philosophy of Black Power. The statement said blacks had the right to lead their own groups and make their own decisions. Perhaps surprisingly, it also said that whites, even those working with SNCC, sometimes intimidated them, a factor that had sometimes made it hard for some blacks to work with whites:

> Negroes in this country have never been allowed to organize themselves because of white interference. As a result of this, the stereotype has been reinforced that blacks cannot organize themselves. The white psychology that blacks have to be watched, also reinforces this stereotype. Blacks, in fact, feel intimidated by the presence of whites, because of their knowledge of the power that whites have over their lives. . . . A climate has to be created whereby blacks can express themselves. The reasons that whites must be excluded is not that one is anti-white, but because the effects that one is trying to achieve cannot succeed because whites have an intimidating effect.

Student Nonviolent Coordinating Committee (SNCC). "The Basis of Black Power." Position Paper, 1966. www.crmvet.org/docs/blackpwr.htm.

merely for the vote, not for some vague kind of freedom, not for legal rights, but the basic force in any society—power. Power for black people, black power."[89]

Before the year had ended, the new ideal had led SNCC to repudiate one of its founding tenets—one that could be seen in the SNCC symbol of two hands shaking, one white and one black. At a SNCC meeting in December in upstate New York, black members decided whites could continue working for SNCC but could no longer vote on decisions the group made. Bill Ware, who headed a SNCC project in Atlanta, said Black Power meant that blacks should be the only ones deciding their future: "Black People and [SNCC] do not understand the concept of black power [because if they did] there would be no white people in the organization at this time."[90]

Bob Zellner, who had been jailed eighteen times in seven states and risked his life for SNCC time and again, was furious and declared: "I will not accept any sort of restrictions or special categories because of race. We do not expect other people to do that in this country and I will not accept it for myself."[91] Despite Zellner's powerful and emotional argument, blacks voted to restrict the rights of white members, and all but seven of forty whites left SNCC.

Commenting on his defeat years later, Lewis said: "What happened that night, was the beginning of the end of SNCC. Cracks were created, wounds were opened that never were healed. [It] was a very sad thing, a tragic thing for SNCC."[92] Lewis's comment was an apt summation of what happened to SNCC in the next few years.

It was Stokely Carmichael, shown here speaking in California, who made the phrase "Black Power" popular. It was supposed to mean power for poor black people, but the phrase quickly became politicized.

SNCC Fades Away

Under Carmichael and H. Rap Brown, who succeeded him as chairman in 1967, SNCC repudiated another of its beliefs—nonviolence, a concept its founders believed was so important that they included it in the group's name. Thanks in great part to SNCC, many types of racial discrimination had ended by 1966, and new federal laws like the Voting Rights Act of 1965 had restored civil rights to blacks. Despite those successes, blacks were still being subjected to racial violence, even those living in big cities like New York, Chicago, and Los Angeles, and were often treated brutally by law enforcement officers.

In explaining why blacks had the right to fight back against violent whites, Brown used inflammatory rhetoric that frightened even whites who supported black rights. At a SNCC rally in July 1967 in Cambridge, Maryland, Brown, who once famously claimed, "Violence is as American as cherry pie," advised blacks to arm themselves and warned whites: "If America doesn't come around, then black people are going to burn it down."[93] Not long after Brown's speech, violence broke out in Cambridge. Police exchanged gunfire with local residents, fire destroyed a black elementary school, and many of the city's black-owned businesses were damaged. Brown was arrested on a charge of inciting to riot because police believed his comments ignited the violence.

SNCC took another radical step in January 1968 when Forman went to Los Angeles and established contact with the Black Panther Party. The Panthers, a militant group founded in Oakland in 1966, armed themselves for protection against racist whites, something that went against SNCC's tradition of nonviolence. The group also established social programs to help blacks and adopted communist views on wealth and social issues. Although Forman was now only an adviser to SNCC, according to Lewis, he was "still the most influential person in Snick. . . . He can tell them to do something, and they will do it."[94] Forman admired the militant Panthers because he believed they were trying to accomplish the same goal that inspired him to fight for civil rights. "[I had] wanted to help create a mass consciousness that we as a people [could use] to fight with our own resources and strengths inside the United States against the injustices that confronted

SNCC Opposes the Vietnam War

———————■———————

SNCC's move toward pursuing more radical ideals actually began in 1966 when the group spoke out against U.S. involvement in the Vietnam War. SNCC issued the following statement on January 6, 1966, while John Lewis was still chairman, just two days after Sammy Younge had been killed in Tuskegee, Alabama:

> The murder of [Younge] is no different than the murder of peasants in Vietnam, for both Younge and the Vietnamese sought, and are seeking, to secure the rights guaranteed them by law. In each case, the United States government bears a great part of the responsibility for these deaths.[1]

Many other groups and some elected officials opposed the war but SNCC's statement angered the federal government, which was struggling to deal with a massive antiwar backlash that was developing throughout the nation. Forman has claimed that SNCC's opposition to the war was a major reason why the U.S. Defense Department in 1967 issued a statement criticizing the group. Citing SNCC's decisions to expel whites and renounce nonviolence, the Defense Department declared that "the switch changed SNCC from the traditional-type civil rights organization to a militant anti-white hate group."[2] The statement failed to note that the Black Power concept, while boosting black pride and self-reliance, did not recommend hating whites.

1. Student Nonviolent Coordinating Committee. Statement on Vietnam, January 6, 1966. www.crmvet .org/docs/snccviet.htm.
2. Quoted in African American Involvement in the Vietnam War. "Student Non-Violent Coordinating Committee (SNCC)," 1967. www.aavw.org/protest/carmichael_sncc_abstract06_full.html.

us,"[95] he said. Forman tried to get SNCC to work closely with the Panthers, but the collaboration failed after several months.

SNCC had accomplished great things in the battle for civil rights since its formation in 1960. But its new Black Power stance and flirtation with the violent Panthers eroded the respect other civil rights groups had held for it. SNCC declined as a power in the fight for black equality and in a few years went out of existence.

In his years at SNCC, Forman had been content to stay in the background. But after SNCC's demise, he became better known than ever through his activities in fighting for black equality.

Black Reparations

Forman said that when he was a child he was so in love with the written word that "I decided if I had to get a job [as an adult] I wanted to get a job dealing with words."[96] Forman never published his novel about civil rights, but after he left SNCC in 1968 *Sammy Younge Jr.: The First Black College Student to Die in the Black Liberation Movement* was published. The book centered on Younge's death and the ongoing civil rights struggle southern blacks were waging.

As Forman started winding down his SNCC activities, he also began reading books about various political and economic theories. His studies led Forman to begin fighting for economic equality for blacks as well as legal equality. In 1969 he became involved with the League of Revolutionary Black Workers, a union movement that sought to better economic and working conditions for blacks. In July 1969, Forman attended the National Black Economic Conference in Detroit, which was sponsored by the Interreligious Foundation for Community Organizations. The group represented Protestant, Catholic, Jewish, black, and other community groups concerned about the lack of economic opportunity for blacks.

At the conference Forman introduced his "Black Manifesto," a detailed paper in which he demanded that white churches pay half a billion dollars to blacks as reparations for previous exploitation by whites. A month later, Forman interrupted a service at New York's Riverside Church to read the manifesto again. The main thrust of his paper was that whites needed to repair the harm racism had done to blacks since the first Africans had arrived as slaves in 1619 in the land that would become the United States. "For centuries we [blacks] have been forced to live as colonized people inside the United States, victimized by the most vicious, racist system in the world. . . . We are demanding $500,000,000 from the Christian white churches and the Jewish synagogues. This total comes to 15 dollars per n****r."[97]

The demand in Forman's manifesto was a new version of "black reparations," the idea that the nation should give blacks some compensation for the misery they had experienced for centuries due to slavery and racism. Forman said the money could be used to help blacks economically in a variety of ways, including

James Forman speaks about the demand for $500 million for reparations for blacks at the National Black Economic Development Conference in 1969.

the creation of a fund to help black farmers who had been evicted from their homes by racist whites for fighting for their rights. Other monies would go to providing blacks more educational opportunities and helping them get better jobs. Even though Forman said years later that "we got tremendous response, tremendous favorable response to it,"[98] the request was never met. Some white religious organizations, however, did contribute several hundred thousand dollars to various black groups to accomplish some of the manifesto's goals.

A Black Revolutionary

The first thing Forman did after leaving SNCC was to go back to school. He completed work on his master's degree in African and African American Studies at Cornell University and in 1982 received a PhD in the same field from the Union of Experimental Colleges and Universities with the Institute for Policy Studies in Washington, D.C. Forman also continued writing, and in 1972 *The Making of Black Revolutionaries* was published. It was both an autobiography that described how Forman's early life forged him into someone willing to dedicate his life to fighting for civil rights and a concise history of SNCC.

Forman moved to Washington, D.C., in 1981 and started the *Washington Times* newspaper. The publication was only in existence a short time, as was the Black American News Service, which he also began. In 1982, Forman helped organize a march that took place on the twentieth anniversary of the historic 1963 civil rights march in Washington. One of the speakers on August 27, 1983, was former SNCC chairman Marion Barry, who had since become mayor of Washington, who loudly proclaimed: "We've had enough! Enough. Enough! We're not going to take it anymore."[99] One major theme of the march was economic equality for poor people, most of whom struggled financially because of racial and other types of discrimination.

In 1990 Forman ran unsuccessfully as a Democrat for senator from the District of Columbia; the election was part of the movement that sought statehood for the district. He later founded James Forman and Associates, a political consulting group, and during the 1990s taught at American University, the University of the District of Columbia, and Morgan State

James Forman speaks at a Martin Luther King Day celebration in 2004.
He remained active in civil rights until his death in 2005.

University in Baltimore. Forman in July 2004 went to Boston
during the Democratic National Convention despite being weak
from a long struggle with colon cancer. He participated in a
protest in which convention delegates from Washington, D.C.,
threw tea bags into Boston Harbor to protest the district's lack
of voting rights in Congress. They were mimicking the Boston
Tea Party of 1773 in which British colonists had protested their
lack of political power. Only seven months later, on January
10, 2005, Forman died at the Washington House, a hospice in
Washington, D.C.

Honored in Death

When Forman died, his fellow Snicks praised him for his wisdom, courage, and organizational genius in the fight for civil rights. Award-winning journalist George E. Curry wrote, "Jim Forman, always dressed in overalls and often puffing on a pipe, was the resident sage of SNCC."[100] Eleanor Holmes Norton, who was at that time a delegate to Congress from Washington, D.C., said Forman was key to SNCC's success: "Jim performed an organizational miracle in holding together a loose band of nonviolent revolutionaries who simply wanted to act together to eliminate racial discrimination and terror."[101] SNCC members from around the nation gathered in Washington to celebrate Forman's life. The memorial program included a Forman quote that summed up his

James Forman's Family

James Forman's sons Chaka and James Jr. donated his papers to the Library of Congress. In a ceremony on January 28, 2008, Librarian of Congress James H. Billington said, "We are proud and grateful to remember this remarkable man. The James Forman Papers are a valuable addition to the Library's unrivaled resources for the study of the 20th-century Civil Rights Movement."

Also attending the ceremony was their mother, Constancia Romilly. Forman met Romilly while she worked with the Student Nonviolent Coordinating Committee. Romilly was white. Her mother was Jessica Mitford, an author, journalist, and political activist who was born in Washington, D.C. Her father was Esmond Romilly, a nephew by marriage to former British prime minister Winston Churchill. Forman's relationship with Romilly began after he had divorced his second wife, Mildred, in 1965. Forman and Romilly never married. James Robert Lumumba Forman, who was born in 1967 and uses the name James Forman Jr., is a professor at Yale Law School. Chaka Esmond Fanon Forman was born in 1970 and is an actor.

Quoted in Helen Dalrymple and Gail Fineberg. "James Forman, Activist; Children Donate Civil Rights Leader's Papers." *Library of Congress Information Bulletin*, March 2008. www.loc.gov/loc/lcib/0803/forman.html.

lifelong fight for racial and economic justice: "Time is short, and we do not have much time and it is time we stop mincing words. No oppressed people ever gained their liberation until they were ready to fight."[102]

Forman, to the end, had been the black revolutionary he described in his book.

Notes

Introduction: SNCC's Organizer

1. Howard Zinn. *SNCC: The New Abolitionists*. Boston: Beacon, 1964, pp. 1–2.

2. Quoted in Jon Meacham, ed. *Voices in Our Blood: America's Best on the Civil Rights Movement*. New York: Random House, 2001, p. 269.

3. Clayborne Carson. *In Struggle: SNCC and the Black Awakening of the 1960s*. Cambridge, MA: Harvard University Press, 1981, p. 31.

4. Quoted in Joe Holley. "Civil Rights Leader James Forman Dies." *Washington Post*, January 11, 2005. www.washingtonpost.com/wp-dyn/articles/A1621-2005Jan11.html.

5. George E. Curry. "The Making of Jim Forman." *New York Amsterdam News*, January 20, 2005, p. 13.

Chapter One: James Forman

6. Quoted in Douglas Martin. "James Forman Dies at 76; Was Pioneer in Civil Rights." *New York Times*, January 12, 2005. www.nytimes.com/2005/01/12/obituaries/12forman_LEDE.html?_r=1&pagewanted=print&position=.

7. James Forman. "My Childhood." National Visionary Leadership Project: Oral History Archive Video Clips. www.visionaryproject.com/formanjames/.

8. Forman. "My Childhood."

9. James Forman. *The Making of Black Revolutionaries*. Seattle: University of Washington Press, 2000, p. 29.

10. James Forman. "Becoming an Honor Student." National Visionary Leadership Project: Oral History Archive Video Clips. www.visionaryproject.com/formanjames/.

11. Quoted in Fred Powledge. *Free At Last? The Civil Rights Movement and the People Who Made It*. Boston: Little Brown, 1991, p. 84.

12. Quoted in LeiLani Dowell. "James Forman Civil Rights Activist. *Worker's World*, February 5, 2005. www.workers.org/2005/forman0203.php.

13. Forman. *The Making of Black Revolutionaries*, p. 11.

14. Quoted in Civil Rights Movement Veterans. "1960: Fayette County TN Tent City for Evicted Voters (1959-1965). www.crmvet.org/tim/timhis59.htm#1959fctc.

Chapter Two: Sit-ins and SNCC

15. Quoted in Thomas R. Brooks. *Walls Come Tumbling Down: A History of the Civil Rights Movement*,

1940–1970. Englewood Cliffs, NJ: Prentice Hall, 1974, p. 146.

16. Quoted in Civil Rights Movement Veterans. "1960: The Greensboro Sit-ins (Feb). www.crmvet.org/tim /timhis60.htm.

17. Quoted in Joanne Grant. *Ella Baker: Freedom Bound*. New York: John Wiley & Sons, 1998, p. 131.

18. Quoted in Brooks. *Walls Come Tumbling Down*, p. 147.

19. Quoted in Henry Hampton and Steve Fayer, eds. *Voices of Freedom: An Oral History of the Civil Rights Movement from the 1950s Through the 1980s*. New York: Bantam Books, 1990, p. 57.

20. Quoted in Faith S. Holsaert et al., eds. *Hands on the Freedom Plow: Personal Accounts by Women in SNCC*. Urbana: University of Illinois, 2010, p. 42.

21. Quoted in Civil Rights Movement Veterans. "1960. Tallahassee Students Gassed & Arrested (Feb–Mar). www.crmvet.org/tim /timhis60.htm.

22. Quoted in Andrew B. Lewis. *The Shadows of Youth: The Remarkable Journey of the Civil Rights Generation*. New York: Hill and Wang, 2009, p. 12.

23. Student Nonviolent Coordinating Committee Founding Statement. www.crmvet.org/docs/sncc1.htm.

24. Quoted in Public Broadcasting Service. *The American Experience*. "Eyes on the Prize: America's Civil Rights Movement, 1954–1985; 'Ain't Scared of Your Jails' (1960–1961)." www.pbs.org/wgbh/amex/eyeson theprize/about/pt_103.html.

25. Quoted in Matthew Pitt. "A Civil Rights Watershed in Biloxi, Mississippi." *Smithsonian*, April 20, 2010. www.smithsonianmag.com/ history -archaeology/A-Civil-Rights-Water shed-in-Biloxi-Mississippi.html.

26. Quoted in Civil Rights Veterans. "A 2003 Interview. Durham, NC, Sit-ins & Protests (1960-61). www .crmvet.org/tim/timhis60.htm.

27. Quoted in *Jackson (MS) Advocate*. "Freedom Riders, Tougaloo Nine Reflect on Great Events of 1961." www.jacksonadvocateonline. com/?p=5955.

28. Quoted in Clayborne Carson et al. *The Eyes on the Prize Civil Rights Reader: Documents, Speeches, and Firsthand Accounts from the Black Freedom Struggle, 1954–1990*. New York: Penguin, 1991, p. 120.

Chapter Three: Freedom Riders and James Forman

29. Quoted in Aldon D. Morris. *The Origins of the Civil Rights Movement: Black Communities Organizing for Change*. New York: Free Press, 1984, p. 232.

30. Quoted in Hampton and Fayer. *Voices of Freedom*, p. 82.

31. Quoted in Civil Rights Movement Veterans. "Freedom Rides (May–Nov)." www.crmvet.org/tim/timhis 61.htm.

32. Quoted in Civil Rights Movement Veterans. "Freedom Rides of 1961." www.crmvet.org/riders/freedom _rides.pdf.

33. Jim Forman. "A Band of Brothers, a Circle of Trust." Internal document written by SNCC executive secretary Jim Forman and distributed at the Waveland, Mississippi, staff retreat of November 1964. www .crmvet.org/nars/forman1.htm.

34. Forman. *The Making of Black Revolutionaries*, p. 223.

35. Quoted in Powledge. *Free At Last?* Boston: Little, Brown, 1991, p. 257.

36. Quoted in "Tributes to and Memories of Jim Forman (1928–2005)." Civil Rights Movement Veterans. www.crmvet.org/mem/forman .htm.

37. Quoted in Carson. *In Struggle*, p. 69.

38. Quoted in Cheryl Lynn Greenberg. *A Circle of Trust: Remembering SNCC*. New Brunswick, NJ: Rutgers University Press, 1998, p. 89.

39. Grant. *Ella Baker*, p. 140.

40. Quoted in Greenberg. *A Circle of Trust*, p. 82.

Chapter Four: SNCC and Voter Registration

41. Carson. *In Struggle*, p. 66.

42. Quoted in Lewis. *The Shadows of Youth*, p. 113.

43. Quoted in Lynne Olson. *Freedom's Daughters: The Unsung Heroines of the Civil Rights Movement from 1830 to 1970*. New York: Scribner, 2001, p. 203.

44. Quoted in Powledge. *Free At Last?*, p. 417.

45. Quoted in Forman. *The Making of Black Revolutionaries*, p. 251.

46. Quoted in Civil Rights Movement Veterans. "Civil Rights Movement: History & Timeline, 1961. Albany GA, Movement (Oct 1961–Aug 1962)." www.crmvet.org/tim/tim his61.htm#1961albany.

47. Olson. *Freedom's Daughters*, p. 231.

48. Quoted in Carson. *In Struggle*, p. 61.

49. Slater King. "The Bloody Battleground of Albany." *Freedomways*, no. 1, 1964. www.crmvet.org/info /sking.htm.

50. Quoted in Carson. *In Struggle*, p. 81.

51. Quoted in Clayborne Carson, ed. *"The Student Voice," 1960–1965: Periodical of the Student Nonviolent Coordinating Committee*. Westport, CT: Greenwood, 1990, p. 84.

52. Forman. *The Making of Black Revolutionaries*, p. 372.

53. Quoted in Bruce Watson. *Freedom Summer: The Savage Season That Made Mississippi Burn and Made America a Democracy*. New York: Viking, 2010, p. 64.

54. Quoted in Juan Williams. *Eyes on the Prize: America's Civil Rights Years, 1954–1965*. New York: Viking, 1987, p. 230.

55. Quoted in John Dittmer. *Local People: The Struggle for Civil Rights in Mississippi*. Urbana: University of Illinois Press, 1994, p. 268.

Chapter Five: Selma, Alabama, and Sammy Younge Jr.

56. Quoted in Greenberg. *A Circle of Trust*, p. 90.

57. Quoted in David Halberstam. *The Children*. New York: Random House, 1998, p. 428.

58. Quoted in Zinn. *SNCC*, p. 165.

59. Quoted in Herb Boyd. *We Shall Overcome*. Naperville, IL: Sourcebooks, 2005, p. 91.

60. Quoted in John Lewis with Michael D'Orso. *Walking with the Wind: A Memoir of the Movement*. New York: Simon & Schuster, 1998, p. 315.

61. Quoted in Carson et al. *The Eyes on the Prize Civil Rights Reader*, p. 218.

62. Quoted in Sheyann Webb and Rachel West Nelson. *Selma, Lord, Selma: Childhood Memories of the Civil-Rights Days as Told to Frank Skiora*. Tuscaloosa: University of Alabama Press, 1980, p. 97.

63. Quoted in Carson et al. *The Eyes on the Prize Civil Rights Reader*, p. 269.

64. Quoted in Vanessa Murphree. *The Selling of Civil Rights: The Student Nonviolent Coordinating Committee and the Use of Public Relations*. New York: Routledge, 2006, p. 134.

65. James Forman. *Sammy Younge Jr.: The First Black College Student to Die in the Black Liberation Movement*. New York: Grove, 1968, p. 25.

66. Forman. *The Making of Black Revolutionaries*, pp. 158–159.

Chapter Six: Life as a Snick

67. Quoted in Lawrence Van Gelder. "Cordell Hull Reagon, Civil Rights Singer, Dies at 53." *New York Times*, November 19, 1996. www.nytimes.com/1996/11/19/us/cordell-hull-reagon-civil-rights-singer-dies-at-53.html.

68. Quoted in Carson. *In Struggle*, p. 82.

69. Quoted in Howard Zinn. *A People's History of the United States: 1492 to Present*. New York: HarperCollins, 1990, p. 453.

70. Quoted in Lewis. *The Shadows of Youth*, p. 5.

71. Quoted in Carson et al. *The Eyes on the Prize Civil Rights Reader*, p. 129.

72. Danny Lyon. *Memories of the Southern Civil Rights Movement*. Chapel Hill: University of North Carolina Press, 1992, p. 30.

73. Quoted in Morris. *The Origins of the Civil Rights Movement*, p. 208.

74. Quoted in Hampton and Fayer. *Voices of Freedom*, p. 145.

75. Quoted in Carson et al. *The Eyes on the Prize Civil Rights Reader*, p. 170.

76. Quoted in Civil Rights Movement Veterans. "The Importance of SNCC: A Discussion," February 2008. www.crmvet.org/disc/sncc.htm.

77. Quoted in *The Student Voice.* "They Lived in the Counties," vol. 3, no. 3, October 1962, p. 1. www.jsums.edu/hamer.institute/resources/Hamer%20Suggested%20Readings/The%20Student%20Voice.pdf.

78. Quoted in Watson. *Freedom Summer*, p. 126.

79. Quoted in Olson. *Freedom's Daughters*, p. 157.

80. Lewis with D'Orso. *Walking with the Wind*, p. 309.

81. Quoted in Lyon. *Memories of the Southern Civil Rights Movement*, p. 63.

82. Quoted in Olson. *Freedom's Daughters*, p. 186.

83. Quoted in Holsaert et al. *Hands on the Freedom Plow*, p. 361.

84. Quoted in Olson. *Freedom's Daughters*, p. 333.

85. Quoted in Charles E. Cobb. "Standing on My Sisters' Shoulders." The Root, November 9, 2010. www.theroot.com/views/standing-my-sisters-shoulders.

86. Quoted in Carson. *In Struggle*, p. 76.

Chapter Seven: SNCC and Black Power

87. Forman. *The Making of Black Revolutionaries*, p. 456.

88. Quoted in Rupert Colley. *Black History: History in an Hour.* New York: HarperCollins, 2011, p. 35.

89. Forman. *The Making of Black Revolutionaries*, p. 457.

90. Quoted in Carson. *In Struggle*, p. 240.

91. Quoted in Lyon. *Memories of the Southern Civil Rights Movement*, p. 179.

92. Quoted in Brooks. *Walls Come Tumbling Down*, p. 266.

93. Quoted in *Time*, "Cherry Pie," October 25, 1971, p. 21.

94. Quoted in Gene Roberts. "Black Power Idea Long in Planning, S.N.C.C. Dissidents Wrote Document Last Winter." *New York Times*, August 5, 1966. http://partners.nytimes.com/library/national/race/080566race-ra.html.

95. Forman. *The Making of Black Revolutionaries*, p. 527.

96. Forman. "Becoming an Honor Student."

97. James Forman. "Black Manifesto." *New York Review of Books*, July 10, 1969. www.nybooks.com/articles/archives/1969/jul/10/black-manifesto/?pagination=false.

98. James Forman. "Response to Reparations." National Visionary Leadership Project: Oral History Archive Video Clips. www.visionaryproject.com/formanjames/.

99. Quoted in Lerone Bennett Jr. "We Still Have a Dream." *Ebony*, November 1983, p. 158.

100. Quoted in Curry. "The Making of Jim Forman," p. 13.

101. Quoted in Joe Holley. "Civil Rights Activist James Forman Dies at 76; Key Organizer of SNCC." *Washington Post*, January 12, 2005. www.washingtonpost.com/wp-dyn/articles/A2403-2005Jan11.html.

102. Quoted in Robert E. Pierre. "Civil Rights Activists Reunite at Memorial." *Washington Post*, February 6, 2005. www.washingtonpost.com/wp-dyn/articles/A1761-2005Feb5.html.

Chronology

1928

James Forman is born in Chicago on October 4.

1960

February 1: Four North Carolina Agricultural and Technical College students begin a sit-in at a Woolworth's lunch counter in Greensboro when they are refused service; the sit-in tactic quickly spreads throughout the South as other college students do the same thing.

April 15–17: During the Easter weekend more than three hundred black and white students meeting at Shaw University in Raleigh, North Carolina, decide to organize as the Student Nonviolent Coordinating Committee (SNCC) to better coordinate the sit-ins.

May 10: White businesses in Nashville, Tennessee, open their lunch counters to blacks, one of many victories resulting from the sit-ins.

1961

May 4: Black and white Freedom Riders leave Washington, D.C., in two buses in an attempt to desegregate interstate buses and bus facilities.

May 14: Racist whites at bus stations in Anniston and Birmingham, Alabama, injure so many riders that the ride is discontinued.

May 20: College students recruited by Diane Nash, a SNCC founder, restart the rides in Birmingham, setting off several months of Freedom Rides that culminate in new federal enforcement policies regarding desegregation of interstate travel.

September: James Forman accepts the position of executive secretary of SNCC.

1963

June: Bernard Lafayette Jr. and his wife, Colia, go to Selma, Alabama, to begin a SNCC voter registration drive.

October 7: SNCC holds a Freedom Day; SNCC workers are arrested for trying to help voters register.

1964

Summer: During the Mississippi Summer Project, sponsored by an alliance of civil rights groups, SNCC provides financing, leadership, and training to one thousand college students who work in a massive voter registration project marred many times by violence, including the murder of three men on June 21.

1965

January 2: A speech by the Rev. Martin Luther King. Jr. ignites a series of protests and marches to boost voter registration in Selma.

March 7: Law enforcement officials and civilian posses attack marchers while they are attempting to march from Selma to Montgomery, Alabama, ending the march; a second march on March 21 succeeds.

March 14: President Lyndon B. Johnson proposes the Voting Rights Act of 1965; Congress approves it on August 6.

1966

May 14–15: In Kingston, Tennessee, SNCC members elect Stokely Carmichael chairman and Ruby Doris Smith executive secretary.

June 16: In Greenwood, Mississippi, SNCC chairman Carmichael uses the term *Black Power* in a speech, popularizing the phrase.

December: SNCC decides that whites can work in the group but no longer have voting rights.

1967

July: In Cambridge, Maryland, SNCC chairman H. Rap Brown threatens violence by blacks if they are not treated better.

1968

Forman leaves SNCC and publishes book on the murder of Sammy Younge Jr.

1969

July: Forman introduces his "Black Manifesto," which demands financial reparations for blacks for damages caused by the nation's past racism.

2005

James Forman dies in a hospice in Washington, D.C., on January 10.

For More Information

Books

Clayborne Carson. *In Struggle: SNCC and the Black Awakening of the 1960s.* Cambridge, MA: Harvard University Press, 1981. The author provides an informative look at the internal struggles in the Student Nonviolent Coordinating Committee.

James Forman. *The Making of Black Revolutionaries.* Seattle: University of Washington Press, 1997. In this autobiography, Forman describes how racism made him fight for black civil rights and chronicles his time with the Student Nonviolent Coordinating Committee.

James Forman. *Sammy Younge Jr.: The First Black College Student to Die in the Black Liberation Movement.* New York: Grove, 1968. Forman describes the death of Younge, a Student Nonviolent Coordinating Committee worker, as it related to the fight for civil rights.

Joanne Grant. *Ella Baker: Freedom Bound.* New York: John Wiley & Sons, 1998. A biography of the woman who helped start the Student Nonviolent Coordinating Committee.

Cheryl Lynn Greenberg. *A Circle of Trust: Remembering SNCC.* New Brunswick, NJ: Rutgers University Press, 1998. The author interviews Student Non-violent Coordinating Committee members for this history of the civil rights group.

Henry Hampton and Steve Fayer, eds. *Voices of Freedom: An Oral History of the Civil Rights Movement from the 1950s Through the 1980s.* New York: Bantam Books, 1990. Members of the Student Nonviolent Coordinating Committee and other civil rights workers tell their stories in their own words about what it was like to fight for civil rights.

Andrew B. Lewis, *The Shadows of Youth: The Remarkable Journey of the Civil Rights Generation.* New York: Hill and Wang, 2009. The author explains how young people became the driving force in the fight for civil rights.

John Lewis with Michael D'Orso. *Walking with the Wind: A Memoir of the Movement.* New York: Simon & Schuster, 1998. The autobiography of John Lewis, perhaps the most famous member of the Student Nonviolent Coordinating Committee.

Danny Lyon. *Memories of the Southern Civil Rights Movement.* Chapel Hill: University of North Carolina Press, 1992. Lyon, a white college student, provides a personal portrait of what it was like to be staff photographer for the Student Nonviolent Coordinating Committee.

Lynne Olson. *Freedom's Daughters: The Unsung Heroines of the Civil Rights Movement from 1830 to 1970.* New York: Scribner, 2001. The author portrays some of the female members of the Student Nonviolent Coordinating Committee, as well as many other women civil rights activists, and their experiences fighting for civil rights.

Howard Zinn. *SNCC: The New Abolitionists.* Boston: Beacon, 1964. This excellent early history of the Student Nonviolent Coordinating Committee is by a college history professor who was an adviser to the group.

Websites

Civil Rights Movement Veterans (www.crmvet.org). This site offers a detailed history of the Student Nonviolent Coordinating Committee, including facts, photos, and personal stories of those involved.

Eyes on the Prize: America's Civil Rights Movement, 1954–1985. "Bridge to Freedom (1965)" (www .pbs.org/wgbh/amex/eyesontheprize /about/pt_106.html). Part of the PBS series *The American Experience*, this site provides a transcript of the episode of the acclaimed television series on the civil rights battle in the mid-1960s in Selma, Alabama, plus links to other information about that important event.

Eyes on the Prize: America's Civil Rights Movement, 1954–1985. "Freedom Summer 1964" (www.pbs.org/wg bh/amex/eyesontheprize/story/09 _summer.html). Part of the PBS series *The American Experience*, this site provides pictures, stories, and links to other sites about the voter registration drive in Mississippi during the summer of 1964.

National Visionary Leadership Project (www.visionaryproject.org/forman james). This site has a biography of James Forman and short videos of Forman discussing fifteen different topics.

We'll Never Turn Back (www.crmvet .org/tim/timhome.htm). An interactive timeline/history of the civil rights movement from 1951 to 1968, including extensive information on the Student Nonviolent Coordinating Committee.

Who Speaks for the Negro? (http://who speaks.library.vanderbilt.edu/interview /james-forman). Robert Penn Warren's archival collection on James Forman provides transcripts of interviews Warren did with Forman for his 1965 book on race relations and civil rights of the same title.

Index

Picture Credits

About the Author

Michael V. Uschan has written ninety books, including *Life of an American Soldier in Iraq*, for which he won the 2005 Council for Wisconsin Writers Juvenile Nonfiction Award. It was the second time he had won the award. Mr. Uschan began his career as a writer and editor with United Press International, a wire service that provides stories to newspapers, radio, and television. Journalism is sometimes called "history in a hurry," and Uschan considers writing history books a natural extension of the skills he developed in his many years as a journalist. He and his wife, Barbara, reside in the Milwaukee suburb of Franklin, Wisconsin.